New Village

A history lesson for the next generation on the
modern Republic of Korea and Park Chung-hee

YOUNG LEE

Also by Young Lee:

Kayak to Serenity

New Dawn

ISBN-13:978-1539 890126
ISBN-10: 1539890120

DEDICATION

To Kim, for fifty years in sickness and in health, for richer or poorer and to our grandchildren Alex, Audrey, and Liam

CONTENTS

ACKNOWLEDGMENTS

I gratefully acknowledge the help and encouragement of many friends and family members. I want to especially acknowledge my wife for her unwavering support and sacrifice. Many friends in New Jersey and Florida also lent their support for my "retirement project" to help those second and third generations of Koreans residing overseas and other readers to learn about Korea and the industrial president Park Chung-hee who ushered in the Miracle on the Han River.

I want to acknowledge the Korean War Veterans Chapter in Delray, Florida for their genuine interest and encouragement. Heartfelt thanks go to the Korean War veterans and friends, Bernard Ruthberg and his wife Sandra, and Barry Tutin and his wife Barbara for their encouragement and their sacrifice in the Korean battlegrounds to save the infant nation with democracy.

Special thanks go to my daughter Jane for help editing and revising the book. I also acknowledge Gregg E. Brickman for her excellent format setting and overall coordination for publishing and Victoria Landis for professional and artistic cover design.

TIMELINE OF MODERN KOREA DURING PARK CHUNG-HEE ERA

Source : **wikipedia.org/wiki/Timeline of Korean history**

Japanese Colonial rule

1916: The final wave of Uibyeong rebels is defeated by Japanese forces

1917: Park Chung-hee was born in Gumi, North Gyeongsang province, Korea—the year added to Wikipedia Timeline

1919: March 1st Movement. Spurred by the sudden and mysterious death of Gojong. Declaration of Korean Independence. Nationwide peaceful demonstrations are crushed by Japanese military and police forces after two months. Governor-General Hasegawa resigns.

1919: The establishment of The Provisional Government of the Republic of Korea in Shanghai.

1919: Saito Makoto appointed as third Governor-General of Korea. The period of "cultural policy" begins.

1920: Battle of Cheongsanri, Korean independence Army, led by Kim Jwa-jin, are victorious.

1926: June 10th Movement.

1932: Korean independence activist Lee Bong Chang fails in his attempt to assassinate Emperor Hirohito in Tokyo.

1932: Korean independence activist Yun Bong Gil bombs Japanese Military gathering in Shanghai.

1938: Governor-General of Korea begins Soshi-kamei (Order to Japanese-style name changes) policy.

1945: The Empire of Japan surrenders to the Allies. According to the terms of Potsdam Declaration, Korea becomes independent.

Division of Korea
1945: After the surrender of Japan, the Korean peninsula is divided between Soviet and American occupation forces at the 38th parallel.

1945: South Korea created a franchise to raise money and funds to recover.

1945: 6 September, Establishment of Peoples Republic of Korea with Yuh Woon-Hyung, but 1946 February, US Army breaks it and Yuh Woon Hyung is murdered.

1946: U.S.-U.S.S.R. Joint-Commission on the formation of a Korean Government reaches an impasse. The Joint-commission is dissolved as the Cold War begins.

1948: 10 May. UN sponsored elections are held in South Korea.

1948: 15 August. Establishment of the Republic of Korea with Syngman Rhee as President.

1948: 9 September. Establishment of the Democratic People's Republic of Korea with Kim Il-sung as Premier.

1949: The murder of Kim Gu. Kim Gu was a Korean independence activist who believed in, and fought for, a unified Korea. He strongly objected to the formation of a separate South Korean state. He was shot in his home by a South Korean Army lieutenant.

1950: 25 June. The Korean War begins.

1950: August. UN Forces are driven back to South-east corner of the Korean Peninsula (The Pusan Perimeter).

1950: September. UN Troops make an Amphibious Landing at Inchon.

1950: November. Chinese Forces enter the war

1953: The Korean War is halted by the Korean Armistice Agreement that has remained in force until now.

1960: A student uprising begins the April Revolution which overthrows the autocratic First Republic of South Korea. Syngman Rhee resigns and goes into exile.

1961: 16 May. Military forces, headed by General Park Chung Hee, overthrow the Second Republic of South Korea in what is known as the Military Coup d'état of 16 May

1961: 12 November. Summit conference for normalization of

Korean-Japanese relations

1962: Start of the first Five-year plans of South Korea

1964: South Korea joins the Vietnam War

1965: 22 June. Signing of Treaty on Basic Relations between Japan and the Republic of Korea. Earned both much controversy and procurement of budgets for later economic developments.

1967: Start of the second Five-year Plan of South Korea

1968: 21 January. An unsuccessful attempt of North Korean commandos to assassinate President Park Chung Hee—the Blue House Raid.

1968: 1 April. Establishment of the Pohang Iron and Steel Company

1968: 5 December. Proclamation of the National Education Charter

1970: 22 April. Start of the government-operated New Community Movement

1970: Gyeongbu Expressway is completed and opened to traffic.

1972: Start of the third Five-year Plan of South Korea

1972: 12 August. The first Red Cross talks between North and South Korea are held

1972: President Park Chung Hee declares Emergency Martial Law and changes Constitution in August, which may allow him to become the permanent ruler. This is similar to Gojong of the Korean Empire stating his country's governmental system is 'autocratic' in the constitution- for greater leadership and less opposition.

1974: 15 August. Assassination of first lady Yuk Young-soo by self-proclaimed North Korean Mun Segwang.

1976: 18 August. The Axe Murder Incident in Panmunjom, Joint Security Area. Triggers former North Korean leader Kim il-sung's first official apology to the South.

1976: 12 October: Discontinuation of rice imports, accomplishment of total self-sufficiency in rice by the 'Unification Rice'

1977: Start of the fourth Five-year Plan of South Korea

1977: 22 December. Celebration of achievement of 10 billion dollars gained by exports

1978: 26 October. Detection of 3rd underground tunnel. Made by North Korea to attack South Korea.

1978: 10 December. Achievement of 1,117 US dollars as GNP.

1979: American president Jimmy Carter visits Korea. Threatens Park by stating he would reduce the U.S. forces in Korea if Park does not stop the ongoing Nuclear Weapons Development project.

1979: 26 October, President Park Chung Hee is assassinated by chief of KCIA, Kim Jaegyu (Assassination of Park Chung Hee).

1979: Coup d'état of December Twelfth, Chun Doo Hwan gets military power

1980: Gwangju massacre. Martial Law is declared throughout the nation. The city of Gwangju becomes a battleground between dissenters and the Armed Forces (18–27 May). Some reports claim over 100 casualties.

INTRODUCTION

Modern Korean history is an important subject as Korea is at a crossroads. On one side is a peaceful unification with North Korea absorbed into South Korea, a democratic economic power. On the other side is a diametrically divided country, a country living under the constant threat of nuclear bombs from communist North Korea under a family dictatorship into its third generation. The historical importance of the moment will double when the communist North has developed the nuclear bomb contrary to the non-proliferation agreement, when sanctions are imposed, and when the political and religious leaders sabotage the government of South Korea, akin to the condition of South Vietnam before the communist takeover.

The search for simple English-language narratives on the subject found no easy answer. The author, having lived in both Korea and the U.S., presents an objective and panoramic view of history through the life of Park Chung-hee (1917-1979), the industrial president who eliminated chronic poverty. The book is essential reading for the second and third generations of Korean immigrants numbering eight million, and world citizens eager to read about the Miracle on the Han River and the New Community Movement President Park ushered in in Korea for a better life and more peaceful world. The book provides ample resources on the military revolution and resulting industrialization, language arts for Koreans and others to learn English, and the inspiration of a charismatic and honest leader who created economic power for peaceful unification of Korea.

PREFACE

Seoul, Korea was my hometown. I was raised and educated there, spending twenty-five of my growing years there. The next fifty years my wife and I found America to be our grateful and loving home country. My time in Korea included living through the brutal fratricidal Korean War in a loving family, my education up to engineering college, mandatory military service as ROTC first class, and a rooky engineering position with Hyundai Corp. The last six years in Korea was during the third republic under Park Chung-hee's revolutionary leadership.

When the 5.16 Revolution by the Korean military erupted in 1961, I was a junior engineering student from a typical poor but loving Korean family. My father lost his assets because a corrupt political lawyer embezzled him out of a home equity loan. I was suspicious of politicians and government leaders. When the grim and intimidating faces of junta leaders showed up in military fatigues, my gut reaction was doubtfulness about the true intention of the revolution and promises for economic progress and national security. As a sensitive young man growing up in the midst of the collective character flaws of Koreans, especially political leaders, acquired from the long colonial and monarchic rule, I had seen the gang mentality of corrupt politicians and so-called elites. I saw the signs of the simple economic rule, "Bad currency drives out good currency," especially in politics.

For example, the founding president Syngman Rhee, who survived long lonely years of independence fighting on the foreign soil of the U.S., was a real leader with courage, education and determination to bridge the Hermit Kingdom under Japan's colonization to a revolutionary republic of democracy and market economy. Instead of respect and support for the wise old leader, his close associates and political leaders put a thick curtain around him to shut his eyes and ears to corruption and election rigging. The student uprising toppled his government. How could this happen to the patriotic, one-race nation? The simple answer is the retention of character defects from colonial years: dishonesty, selfishness, factionalism, bribing, *Han-tang Ju-eui* (one big deal solves everything) and the corrupt the-ends-justifies-the-means attitude.

The breathtaking progress of the bloodless military revolution, the first in a half-millennium of Korean history, was in my peripheral view while I was directing my attention and energy to immediate things like where my tuition would come from, was I fit for the rigorous ROTC summer camp, could I get a decent job after graduation, would I meet a nice girl to marry, how about my ambition to get a doctoral degree in the U.S ? I listened to the revolution pledge repeated at every public function with elation one time and deep doubt another time. How could the revolution succeed when other regimes could not accomplish their goals due to the harsh reality of neither possessing natural resources nor investment capital? Besides, I had the lingering question that even if Park Chung-hee were the Heaven-sent savior of the poorest country, leaders and elites with colonial minds could derail the man and his pledge.

When I left Seoul in the summer of 1967, Korea was one of the poorest countries in the world. Nevertheless, during my six years under Park's government, I saw a subtle but definite change in the political, social and economic fabric of the country. I missed experiencing the changes while starting a new life on foreign American soil but I always desired to see the epochal changes in my motherland. Writing became my retirement project to look back on my life and the two Korean presidents I admire and respect deeply. Maybe, nostalgia makes patriots.

Today, fifty years later in America, at a cozy retirement community, I am engulfed in the life story of Park Chung-hee and the industrialization of Korea to write a short narrative in English for our future generation, especially for those in foreign lands. After watching the miracle on the Han River Park Chung-hee spearheaded, I came to believe, for Koreans, wisdom and patriotism come from learning about the two Presidents Park Chung-hee and Syngman Rhee with a symbiotic relationship. The current situation in Korea is precarious. Nuclear threat from the communist North and the corrupt politicians with devastating colonial minds and communist influence further divide the nation, creating South-Vietnam-like conditions before their communist take-over. The crisis makes it necessary to learn about true patriotism and courage from the honest and charismatic leader's, Park Chung-hee's, life.

I am encouraged to write as I have immediate readers for my book. My three grandchildren, ages eleven to twelve, would benefit from the book for knowing their heritage and meeting a truly great man with honesty, courage, and determination to free millions of people from poverty and defeatism. I also recognize some eight million Koreans spread around the world as immigrants and expatriates may find the book useful to learn about the revolutionary and the economic liberator of Korea. For me, writing on the industrialization president, President Park, is a logical follow-up to my previous book on the Founding President Syngman Rhee.

Some remarkable changes came immediately after the 5.16 Revolution. Law and order had an instant jumpstart with the swift arrest of corrupt politicians responsible for the election rigging and use of street gangs for political purposes. Citizens of Seoul saw a surprise parade of street gangsters with political connections holding large placards to the glee of the long-waiting hard-working citizens. Rule by tough laws came to clean and fertilize the land for economic development and national security. The government's swift establishment of the Economic Planning Board with the U.S.-educated experts provided the theory and plan, and Park added muscle with no possibility of raising the white flag of plan failure. Real economic planning for the sake of Korean people was non-existent during colonial and monarchic rule for generations.

As a college student in Seoul, I saw a strange logic and attitude existed in Korea towards the definition of patriotism. The logic was it was patriotic to leave the country and create opportunity for the people remaining in the overcrowded society where the system of competition and work and rewards were all corrupted with bribes, political connections, factionalism, and cowardice of the leaders. Corrupt politicians surrounded themselves with false witnessing friends, alumni, and subordinates to make their empire of corruption prosecution-free. Under these conditions, fair play was not possible and it was better to pack and leave. Many talented and patriotic people left for they could not expect fair play, reasonableness, and justice. They chose to leave the den of corrupt, cowardly politicians. The colonial minds were everywhere with a smile in the front and a dagger in the back. The only people trustworthy were family and that was why so many family *chaebols* or conglomerates opened their doors in Korea at the time.

Many people left and my Mayflower boat for the promised land was a British Airlines flight from Seoul to New York's Kennedy Airport. I did not flee the country to avoid debts or government obligation. I came to the new world in search of a more perfect world and a better life without exercising the dormant colonial mind to manipulate and take advantage of someone with less means than I had. On leaving my hometown without knowing the future, I wholeheartedly wished the new third republic with Park's leadership would change the old ineffective order with a new order of justice and equality. President Park had the toughest job with starving people on one side and on the other, the ever-provoking communist Kim Il-sung with threats and self-aggrandizing lies of "*Juche*," self-reliance. Kim made the empty promise of "We are one race without need of outsiders," a sweet but murderous message.

The plane that took me from my wife of one month waving at Gimpo Airport landed at Kennedy Airport in New York. I had $50.00 and a two-year engineer trainee contract in my pocket. With the help of my employing company in New Jersey, my wife joined me in three months. I met my wife, a freshman at a teachers' college, by sheer chance when I was an engineering major at SNU. It was love at first sight. We dated for five years before marriage. We worked hard to make the most of the opportunities the free democratic society would offer.

We started to accomplish things we never expected back in Korea. We did not expect anything free as we knew capitalism was not built on give-aways in ration form but was built on the people's ingenuity to help themselves in a free and competitive environment. We marveled at our accomplishments: a used car in six months, a Master's degree in engineering in two years, a three-bedroom dream house in an upscale community in four years, and a Doctoral degree in engineering in seven years, with a dissertation on applying systems theory to transportation engineering. We thought the positive would continue until we realized they were one side of the coin called life. The other side was quite full too. I have two daughters, the older one is a partner at an international law firm, the younger one, the smarter of the two, a psychology graduate and freelancer in life, living single and the frequent subject of my prayers.

Freedom is not free nor is life in the richest country in the world. In my third year in the U.S. I was working full-time and going to school full-time with no time to spare. While preparing for a qualifying examination for a doctoral program, I had occasion to go to a swimming pool at the college with my visiting brother-in-law. I used to go swimming to maintain my health once on the weekends at a pool available free of charge for students and their families. After one hour of swimming, we got out of the pool and got ready to leave. I was puzzled to see my brother-in-law taking time to dry his feet before putting on his sneakers. I did not take time to dry my feet before putting on my sneakers. I could not afford a few minutes of time and that was the system of democracy for individuals responsible for their own goals.

I explored the life of Park Chung-hee with two questions and two objectives. The two questions I had were "Are there real changes in Korea since I left fifty years ago?" and "Is South Korea's economic development and industrialization a convincing catalyst for peaceful unification?" The answer for the first is obvious because people have plenty of food, a higher living standard, and a GDP per capita of over $30,000, offering a modern lifestyle. The GDP at the revolution was $87. Now, is the change of Korean mindset comparable to the physical change? It appears that open and free democracy has been enhanced selectively. Selective in a sense that the rich and powerful and the poor without power do not have the same level of freedom. To one segment of people, it is all freedom without comparable responsibility, to the other segment, it is all responsibility without real economic and political freedom. In a nutshell, the collective character flaws of Koreans retained from the long colonial rule remained or even got worse and it is scary to be reminded of the last parting words of Japanese Resident Governor of Korea, Abe Nobusyuke, in August, 1945,

We lost the war but Korea(Joseon) did not win. I bet it will take far more than a hundred years for Koreans to wake up and restore the great shining old glory of Korea. We, Japan, has implanted colonial education in Koreans' minds much more powerful than guns and artillery. After all, Koreans will betray each other and live like slaves. Look, Korea was really great and glorious but the present Korea will be slaves of colonial education and I, Abe, will return.

My objectives for exploring the life of Park Chung-hee are twofold. One is to warn my hard-working and law-abiding compatriots in Korea that the threat of the communist North is real with their lies, communist followers in the South and now their nuclear threat. The combined effects of colonial minds and communism is deadly. The corrupt politicians, religious leaders and social elites are creating the condition of the defunct South Vietnam before communist takeover and learning about Park Chung-hee is critical. The other objective is to provide a narrative in English for the second and third generations of Koreans spread all over the world and readers with an interest in Korea's industrialization and community movement for a better and more perfect world.

1

BORN IN BLOOD

"Na neun gwen chan ah"

It was the last words president Park Chung-hee uttered before he collapsed forward. Park's trusted aid and confidante Kim Jae-gue had just fired a pistol to his heart. Blood gushed out when Park said his last words calmly and also consolingly, "I am all right."

Park's lifelong attitude towards people other than himself, whether a soldier in his unit or people in his beloved country, was on fine display to show his moral character as a leader.

Two more bullets followed from Kim's second pistol, one to finish off Cha Ji-chul, the chief of the presidential security, and the other aimed at the rear part of Park's head. There was a brief delay due to a malfunction of the first pistol. Park's security head Mr. Cha who attended the dinner with Park's top aides was already lying dead before Park's demise as the attack was directed at Cha first.

Thus, the remarkable political leader's life, his century-old dream of the country's economic independence and the 18 years of ironclad rule, came to a sudden stop in the midst of crimson blood. It poured out from the bodies of the president and his security chief, gunned down in a so-called safe house at the same time on October 26[th,] 1979. Figuratively, what started with a sword ended with a sword, culminating in the life of the most influential and respected, but controversial, political leader in Korean history. Profound economic and social transformation have taken place because of President Park Chung-hee's personal courage and sharp focus to usher in the Miracle of the Han River to the once devastated land of fratricidal war and Japan's colonization for thirty-six years.

"Small peppers are hotter," the plain Korean saying, seemed invented for its application to Park for his physical and facial traits. His short, slender body and bony face appeared devoid of any unnecessary fat and muscles. He seemed to be a hardworking, typical Korean farmer with plenty of work in the field, on the bare minimum diet of barley rice and cheap vegetables. The dark bony face with high cheekbones tended to ooze out the pathetic feeling of malnutrition and helpless poverty, the dominating quality of the farming region in Korea. However, in stark contrast, the shiny dark brown eyes with laser-sharp focus quickly showed the brilliance, determination and dominating power of the person in direct opposition to the bodily depravity.

Park was born in 1917 at the small rural village of Gumi, North Gyeongsang province as the last child of seven siblings, two sisters and five brothers. The house he was born in was a dilapidated farm house with a thatched roof, mud walls and an open entrance. The poor, shabby look of the farmhouse showed the neglect and backwardness of the Korean monarchs' ruling over five hundred years with the Confucian influence of a passive lifestyle without many improvements in the basic life essentials: clothing, food and dwelling. The condition of the housing also showed Japanese colonization and the hardship of deficient life quality living under brutal colonial rule. Japan with its military and national power gained from early westernization, used that power to colonize its neighbor, Korea, with a systematic plan and military might starting in 1905, twelve years before Park's birth. Japan first took away the Korean military and her diplomatic independence in 1905, and then put through the direct annexation in 1910. Imperial Japan had a wild dream of subjugating neighboring countries in Asia using Korea as a springboard.

After annexation, Korea became Japan's supply depot to support its burgeoning expansion of military operations with material and manpower needed for their wild dream of conquering neighbors. Furthermore, the Korean peninsula was their convenient bridge to attack deeper into Manchuria and the rest of the Asian continent. Japan's colonial priority was the security apparatus to control the Korean population and the infrastructure to feed its expanding army with local resources found in Korea. For instance, Korean rice, of a superior quality, was an imminent target as were war materials along with other weapons-manufacturing materials such as iron, copper, tungsten and many more mined raw materials. Under such a forcible system of confiscation, capturing and taxation, the welfare and living condition of rural farmers were far from the goal and concern of the

Japanese colonial government.

The age-old poverty-stricken rural life in Korea persisted and signs of malnutrition and hand-to-mouth living were apparent in rural farming regions. Besides, Park's birth year, 1917, was far from peaceful in the world as the First World War was in its fourth year and many nations and people on both sides of the belligerence had seen many killings, maiming and brutality.

The nationalism with romantic and patriotic fervor wreaked havoc by encouraging the killing of the enemy soldiers and populace with ever sophisticated and deadly weapons including poison gas. For ever-widening conflicts among nations for narrow national interests and power, amicable solutions, especially for smaller countries, did not exist. Woodrow Wilson was the U.S. President, a deeply religious and humanistic man dreaming of world peace and brotherhood without war. As WWI fortunately progressed for the victory of Allied forces, President Wilson was busy preparing for the peace conference at the conclusion of the war. President Wilson, mindful of the predicament of small countries in Asia and Africa desiring independence, wanted to provide leadership in the formation of the League of Nations and proclaimed the principle of self-determination for the New World Order.

The President Wilson happened to understand the agony and frustration of a small colonized country through his meeting with a young and cool but dedicated student from Korea. Syngman Rhee was at Princeton University for his PhD program on international political science and religion when Wilson was the university president. Wilson was immensely impressed by this lonely student for his devotion to work and concern for his mother country's, Korea's, independence. Out of his love and caring for people, especially underdogs, Wilson used to invite Rhee over, the only student from Asia and from a backward country Korea, a continent and an ocean away. A year after Rhee's Princeton enrollment, the first Chinese student came to the institution with a long history. Wilson introduced Rhee at his family and friends gatherings as a savior of Korea, and his prediction was fulfilled some thirty-three years later in 1948. Rhee put his hands on a Bible to start a democratic republic under the untenable condition of two opposing and marauding nations, the communist North Korea and the democratic South.

In the year of 1917 when Park was born during the bloody

colonial occupation, the future founding president Rhee was hard at work in Hawaii. Having completed his bid for his higher education from the renowned universities of George Washington University, Harvard, and Princeton, he was busy developing a network of influential people and organizations in the continental United States with coveted academic degrees of masters, PhD and ordination as a Christian minister. Rhee's previous reform movements in Korea to block colonization by advancing Japanese military power brought him pain, frustration, and sadness, including long-term imprisonment, with a death sentence hanging over his head from the last Korean monarch.

With totally renewed devotion and commitment to Korean independence movements overseas, Rhee worked incessantly. He had profound gratitude for the meager base for his work on Oahu Island, Hawaii, that had a short history of Korean immigrants from the occupied motherland oceans away. The small band of Korean immigrants numbering one hundred-two came to Honolulu on a steamship, the S. S. Gaelic, in 1902, after nurturing and sympathetic work by the American missionaries in Korea. Those missionaries serving at a small congregation in Incheon in rags and on a starvation diet realized a God-given opportunity to link the source of cheap and eager laborers with the big sugar and pineapple plantations in Hawaii needing many dependable workers.

The missionaries were willing and ready to be the go-betweens between the two parties with differences of night and day in culture, behavior, and food with perfect credentials of love, trust and doing God's work. Persuasion to leave the family and the place of birth for a foreign place for a long voyage on a primitive steamship was almost impossible to the naive Confucian followers. Koreans under long Confucian teaching and its influence regarded the separation from family as an improbable adventure and as abandoning filial duty towards their parents and family members. Koreans were, in general, uneducated, passive and very class-sensitive for work as laborers in a foreign country with a different culture, tradition and even a language difficult to learn and speak. For the plantation owners, the go-between missionaries also had an uphill battle as they had inhibitions toward the so-called "savages from the Orient."

The missionaries persisted in their work to narrow the differences and mental blocks of the two groups and finally saw the possibility of having a contractual agreement. The winning approach was devised based on two seemingly basic natures of each party's need and fear. For Korean workers there was nothing much to lose. They would have a chance to make money to send home and in the worst-case scenario, they could return home after the contract had been fulfilled. Besides, they would have one big bonus of having seen the world as a part of their journey, something to brag about when they returned home. For the plant owners, a better alternative was not in sight to have a committed and dependable workforce without fear of strikes and group actions against the owners. Beyond the basic interests and worry each party had, both parties had immense trust in the missionary's honest work and wisdom to create a mutually beneficial contract agreement.

In 1917, another kind of agreement was required to actualize Park's birth in a poor Korean farm family under Japanese colonial rule. The agreement was rather funny and comical. Nonetheless, the parents made a deadly serious and crucial agreement for the precious life in the mother's womb to be born. The agreement was between two parents, the father and the mother, to continue the pregnancy and nurse the baby in the womb with necessary nutrition and life-supporting activities. Pregnancy in a large poor family with seven children was a worry rather than a welcome as it meant another mouth to feed and clothe. It was a psychological and practical burden. Park's mother did not want their seventh child of five brothers and two sisters to be born into a poverty-stricken and declining noble or scholar-class family. On top of this financial concern, the mother was ashamed to have the last baby at her advanced age, 45, at the turn of the century in Confucian culture and society with a female life expectancy of less than fifty years. She was afraid to become a laughingstock expecting a baby at her age when her daughter-in-law was expecting a baby too. The mother had real motivation to have an abortion. A safe abortion by a licensed Western doctor would have been a desired solution. Nevertheless, that approach was out of reach because such a practice was simply impractical for the lack of money and moral reluctance.

The mother had to try other, somewhat natural ways of ending the pregnancy. Now, the mother had ingenuity to cause a natural abortion by engaging in subtle and secretive activities. She started to jump down elevated places believing the gravity would do the trick. At other times, she was walking, running, and massaging with no result. The pregnancy continued and she even tried to drink soy bean sauce that every family used for cooking. Still, no results from the dark black soybean sauce except years later the dark-skinned complexion of the future president attributed its cause to the soybean sauce his mother had consumed. Soon, the hilarious activity stopped as the pregnancy came to be known and loving husband and family support followed.

In 1917, the pressure that permeated from degrading and helpless poverty hit the family and all the peaceful and hardworking general populace. They lived in the cursed land under Japanese occupation and in the backward Confucian monarchy before that. The crushing weight of poverty was everywhere for generations under grossly negligent monarchs, passive Confucian influence and the brutal colonial confiscation. In 1917, poor people of the world also saw the Bolshevik revolution in the vast Russian Empire with Marx-Lenin theory of classless and equal society for land, material and services through government control and rations. The oppressed people in Russia, Europe and beyond the borders saw the revolution as a solution to avenge and correct many centuries-old social divisions of the ruling and ruled under an absolute monarchy like that of the Russian Czar .

The Soviets were formed in 1905 by workers' uprising and eventually came to power through the 1917 October Revolution. Marxist and Leninist ideology pushed one party, the Proletarian Party, with the dictum "the end justifies the means," emphasizing systematic killing of reactionaries and aggressive propaganda tactics luring poor farmers, soldiers and vast ignored people as well as very naive intellectuals dreaming of a perfect world, utopia without class and injustice.

Unfortunately, the seed of communism was planted in the same year of Park's birth and would soon torment Park's family and the future president Park in devastating ways. The ideology of communism divided Korea in the middle along the 38th parallel, causing the most brutal fratricidal war; brothers killing brothers, sons maiming fathers, and students attacking teachers.

In 1950, Park was 33 years old when North Korea invaded

South Korea with Soviet-made tanks and superior weaponry. He was already in the thick of war commanding South Korean units with his long experience in the army and in its leadership. Park's training and experience as a combat duty officer in the Japanese army drew the respect and approval of the army high brass and junior officers as well as soldiers he commanded. Park served in various capacities while the war continued like an ignited bomb because of the Cold War confrontation between democracy and communism. The war was a ferocious civil war started by communist Kim Il-sung of the North desiring unification by force. The war also saw the first U.N. intervention to stop communist aggression in a united way. Park's leadership in the army intelligence units and artillery warfare greatly helped him to launch a precarious military revolution against the corrupt and ineffective government on May 16, 1961, shortly after the students' revolution in 1960.

Communism brought personal tragedy to Park and his family as Park's second older brother, whom he regarded as a mentor, was killed in a communist demonstration during the lawless and confused time before the first South Korean republic was launched in 1948. Park's brother was an educated and intelligent young man during the chaotic time. He was involved in communist activities and was cut down by police forces controlling the pro-communist demonstration. Communism had a very personal dimension for the future president to defend and protect the free and market economy of the republic of Korea.

Closer to the hearts of Koreans under Japanese colonial occupation, the first Korean immigrants to Hawaii in 1902 quietly grew and expanded to provide an immigrant community and financial base for the Korean independence movement led by a few devoted leaders. Syngman Rhee came to Hawaii to start a more meaningful and coordinated independence movement by lecturing at Korean churches and by plunging into the education of immigrants' children and adults for English learning and community networking. The first one-hundred-two Korean immigrants was a meager start to Korean immigrant history. Likewise, the first American Pilgrims brought on the Mayflower who arrived in Cape Cod in November, 1620, after a 66-day voyage also numbered 102 as if the two undertakings were in providence. Mayflower braves crossed the Atlantic Ocean with frequent deadly storms and the Korean explorers crossed the relatively calm Pacific Ocean.

Nevertheless, the crew of the ship and Korean voyagers who were on a steamship for the first time in their life were in shock and dread. The ocean suddenly broke with thundering waves and lightning without any advance warning whatsoever. Both big oceans were tumultuous and frightful for passengers without previous experience to deal with a vast ocean with no end in sight. Every minute, every hour and every day was a challenge for those on the ship yearning for the moment they could step on something solid and not moving. These Korean contract workers endured the perilous voyage well with tight mouths and high hopes. The workers had limited education but a high moral compass to follow through their association with the missionaries.

As the immigrant population increased and settled down, their lives became more routine and expected. They now started to indulge in a more relaxed and exciting lifestyle, taking risks to do morally reprehensible activities like heavy drinking and gambling. These people did not have much recreational outlet because of lack of money and language problems. People got into unlawful and sometimes outright criminal acts like stealing and violent attacks on people. Syngman Rhee in Hawaii with his mission of educating the Korean community was in shock when he saw the younger generation in deep trouble. The second generation, with a bit more financial and social leeway owing to their parents' hard work, forgot their origins and got into trouble with major social and criminal implications. A few of the Korean second-generation became criminal hoodlums, taking advantage of their citizenship and some spent money from their hard working parents without much time to spend with their children. In fact, Rhee found himself in turmoil as gangs of the second generation and newcomers got into serious trouble with the law and were convicted for their crimes. He lamented he could not have been involved earlier in the education and direction of Koreans in Hawaii to prevent them from serious problems. Rhee was in shock and hopeless when a Korean descendant, Yee Yo-keuk, was to be executed in 1917 for his crime of murder and other violent attacks that shook up the Japanese residents on the peaceful Hawaiian Islands.

Syngman Rhee as a preacher and Korean congregations' spiritual leader sat with Yee Yo-keuk the day before his execution for an hour.

Rhee heard Yee repenting and gave him the last Christian service with tears in his eyes. Holding Yee's trembling hands, Rhee realized in a flash the importance of education for Korean immigrants and their second generation. Rhee concluded with renewed conviction that education alone would empower Koreans in Hawaii and those scattered in many countries without a nation. Education was a must for Koreans to be good citizens and to organize a united and more effective Korean independence movement. Education of Koreans in the church organizations and all their learning facilities became Rhee's primary concern. Financial resources from the Korean community were scarce as they came from the pockets of low-paid Korean immigrant laborers. The meager funds were so precious that no one had a free hand to squander them for other purposes.

Rhee attained more financial help from Koreans realizing their youngsters' problem and from the American church he affiliated with to do something for the second generation. Rhee did not lose time in finding a place and founded schools for Korean runaways and problem young girls in Hawaii. He also exerted effort to get the schools accredited by the authorities for the purpose of additional funding and drawing more qualified teaching staff for Koreans' education in English and other important subjects. Often, Rhee got into arguments and even violent confrontation with other Korean community leaders over the use of funds if it was not for education, the priority #1. Rhee did not mind going against church leaders or friends. He even confronted his blood-pledged brother, Pak Yong-man, when Pak diverted funds earmarked for the schools to the Korean Military Academy for young Korean boys in the U.S. Pak's high visibility and patriotic plan was "to hell with good intentions" as far as Rhee was concerned. Rhee contended that it was nice to attack Japanese forces wherever possible by Korean soldiers trained by this blood-brother Pak Yong-man for show and morale boosting. However, Rhee thought military confrontation with Japanese superior forces would be an unnecessary risk with minimal long-term effect. Diversion of the blood money for such a glamour project was a no-no to Rhee and he took over the Korean Association, handling the fundraising and the use of money.

In 1920, the relationship between Rhee and Pak was severed with no chance for brotherhood again. Rhee's uncompromising emphasis on education was long and hard. At first, a few Sunday school teachers volunteered to teach in the borrowed space in American churches. In the later days, more volunteers supported Rhee's aggressive educational policy. Finally, when Rhee became president of South Korea, an all-out national effort was made and resources appropriated to building schools, training teachers and founding an education ministry in the government. Back in the home country an ocean away, Japan had a brutal policy to eradicate Korean culture, language and even Korean names to completely surgically attach two separate nations and races. The grand objective for Japan was a thousand-year rule of Asia and to become the sole master in Eastern civilization.

When Rhee was elected the first President of the Republic of Korea in 1948 and was inaugurated in with his hands on the Bible, Korea was the poorest country in the world and did not have a bright future. The U.S. Undersecretary of State, Dean Acheson said that he did not expect "roses to blossom from a garbage dump." That was an accurate description of Korea at the time. The new government soon started a national policy to select smart students from all fields, especially technical and engineering areas, and send them to advanced educational institutions on government scholarships. The selected students were to go to Western countries like America, France, Germany and more. The national emphasis on education with long vision created fertile soil for the national reconstruction when Park Chung-hee came into power through a bloodless revolution in 1961.

The poor and long-suffering nation saw potential for the first time. The merging of fresh leadership from the military and the educated populous was dramatic to headstart the political, social, economic and industrial changes and rapid progress. Cutting off this cycle of generational poverty and hand-to-mouth existence was the grandest goal for all Koreans. Syngman Rhee's foresight in establishing democracy based on a market economy in the southern half of the Korean peninsula and Park's birth in blood in a poor Korean family were perfect examples of providential design for Korea's economic development.

In 1917, in contrast to the sleepy and backward atmosphere in a Korean farm village at the time of Park's birth, a drastic departure from the conventional wisdom happened in physics. Einstein, 38 years old in 1917, drew worldwide attention to his theory of relativity that broke the concept of absolute space and time of Newton's era.

Einstein's "mind experiment" successfully generated the mind-boggling concept of relativity not in the lab but in the mind. Yet, eventually a physical test took place in the form of "eclipse observation" in 1919 verifying his theory. The theory and the test quickly opened the human mind towards a higher realm of understanding of the universe in which humans exist but forget its presence. Cosmology is a science to understand the universe for its size, history and much other related information. This science is conceptual and elusive but Einstein helped to understand it with his Theory of Relativity. His theory went further to inaugurate exciting new science such as atomic energy, lasers, photo electricity, fiber optics, semiconductors and space travel.

Nevertheless, his real contribution was to see the world and phenomenon in the universe as probabilistic and relative rather than absolute and constant. The theory and the concept have led people to respect free spirit and tolerance in humanity. His famous energy formula $E=MC^{**}2$ showed the power of atomic energy and the power of imagination from which his mind experiments had started for a successful conclusion.

A subtle parallel exists between Einstein and Park Chung-hee, a future revolutionary, in that Park imagined the power of revolution by a dedicated small group of young officers in transforming a poverty-stricken land and its demoralizing 5,000 year history. As a naturalized U.S. citizen, Einstein spent hours in his small sailboat named "Tinef," or "a piece of junk" in Yiddish, at the end of Long Island Sound near the Atlantic Ocean. He would drift aimlessly but think about big things like the universe and its law. Likewise, Park, when grown up, spent much time in or out of his army uniform thinking and dreaming about big things like revolution to change Korean history for the better. Einstein once advised his son by saying that life is like riding a bicycle. To keep his balance, he must keep moving. So was Park moving from one position to another in the Korean army, his chosen universe, to march with young officers and their men for a worthy revolution with patriotic zeal and courage.

Survival is a challenge. It can be a much bigger and insurmountable challenge if you lose freedom and collective protection. As the world changed with the end of World War I in 1918, the year after Park's birth, Koreans under Japanese colonial rule woke up and organized a non-violence movement, the Mansei

11

movement, on March 1, 1919. Now, Koreans, men and women, young and old, started the long struggle for eventual independence in 1945. Park Chung-hee's role in history came to the foreground to change the poor and pathetic economic conditions and the mindset of Koreans to a "can do" spirit.

2

SURVIVAL INSTINCT

"Let's work and fight!"

Survival is a challenge. It is a much bigger and more insurmountable challenge if you lose your freedom and collective protection from your own government. When the future president Park was born, Korea was in the tight shackles of colonial rule imposed with an iron grip on the Korean peninsula by Imperial Japan. Already Japan had a dozen years to perfect their colonial ruling infrastructure such as transportation systems, housing, prisons, schools, and hospitals to govern Korea for a long time, maybe forever.

Although Park Chung-hee had brushes with death many times in his spectacular and epoch-making life, he enjoyed remarkable survival instincts during his sixty-three year life until his life was cut down by his close confidante and follower eight years his junior in the KCIA (Korean Central Intelligence Agency), Kim Jae-gue. Park and Kim came from the same village and attended the same Taegu teachers' school and Korean Military Academy. Because of their age difference, Park was a mentor for him and supported him in his military career. In fact, Park trusted Kim and appointed him to the second most powerful position in the KCIA to protect and sustain Park's presidency. Park's assassination by the trusted subordinate in the inner circle of their governing body clearly indicated the stress and strain of a continued presidency of Park and the Yusin dictatorship without term limits.

Park and Kim had a very long friendly relationship like brothers. Park's assassination by Kim carries a deeper meaning of the two individuals' convictions on different roles and responsibility for the historic event changing the direction of the nation. Park understood his unique role with historical consequence and the fulfillment of his lifelong dream to liberate the nation from the yoke of chronic poverty. Park often reflected on his mother with all the signs of abject poverty in her clothes, in her face and on her body, and her sighs looking at the empty rice bin.

Kim Jae-gyu, Park's totally unexpected assassin, also recognized his unique role for the country with an uncertain future due to the expanding anti-government demonstrations started by students of Busan National University on October 16, 1979. Kim was a soldier and a patriot in his own mind with long military training and his service as a general and a division commander and had courage to risk his life for the service of the fragile country. For the tragic end of their friendship and perceived roles, the two strong minds, their sense of service for the country, and patriotism collided in violence in the utmost sacrificial manner. In his final testimony before the military Court, Kim referred to his action of killing president Park and his security chief, Cha Ji-chul as a revolution for the country and had no remorse for the sad collision with the most powerful principal of the Yusin government and his hometown friend and mentor.

Furthermore, Kim concluded that his lonely revolution had appropriate and patriotic goals. Kim listed five items as revolutionary objectives: recover free democracy, eliminate demonstrator casualties, prevent communist threat, improve Korea – U.S. relationship, and lastly, enhance international image. Kim asserted that, to achieve his noble goal, he did not mind shortening his life for another 10 or 15 years at his age of 55. While delivering his final message in an organized and dignified manner before the military court for a potential death sentence, he said that he did not wish to beg for his life, but implored the court to save the lives of his subordinates as he was solely responsible for the violent action.

President Park had his own sense of duty and role-playing before the assassination. Even though the original bloodless 5.16 Revolution was successful and the third republic and fourth republic were installed, he recognized his mission was not complete. Economic development and industrialization had to come to a successful conclusion to reasonably guarantee the elimination of chronic poverty and strong national self-defense against the communist North. Park's keen awareness as to the need for economic revolution before a realistic rooting of democracy in Korean society made him busy researching and analyzing other comparable political models.

At the time two things were clear to Park. One was the time frame for the required economic development and the industrialization of the nation, and the other was the trustworthiness and readiness of the opposing political parties to assume political power and the continued economic revolution. On the first count of the time requirement, Park's understanding was the time of the revolutionary government under his presidency was not enough to fulfill the economic mandate to eliminate poverty and attain the nation's self defense. Two or three terms of four years were not enough to eliminate absolute poverty. Park gingerly took account of historical models to answer his questions. The models included Japan's Meiji restoration, Lee Kuan Yew of Singapore's political and economic independence, and the Philippines' Ferdinand Marcos' modernization and defense against communism. All took more than two decades with a central government in control and with some sort of autocratic or dictatorial power to take care of the nation's order and continued progress according to the plan of national development. During national development, even though the basic civil rights were provided, a full-scale American style of free democracy was not. It was on hold and in delay for full implementation of the economic revolution.

The time requirement for Korea to create economic revolution was more than other countries needed as Korea had to work and fight the war in armistice against communist North Korea's ever-present threat of invasion. The time and the resources South Korea had had to be divided because of the cold reality of survival. President Park's common sense and his survival instinct living under Japanese colonial rule came in handy as Park declared emergency measures to mobilize all forces in the nation to support the economic revolution in progress. He defended the country with hurriedly-organized village defense corps consisting of retired army veterans and villagers, both men and women. The nation had practically been in a war situation as Kim Il-sung, the communist dictator in the North, discarded the armistice agreement unilaterally.

The communist regime in the North, under the pressure of observing the economy in the South taking off from the bottom with "Export #1 policy," was afraid of their failure of an economic development plan. Low morale and division among the hardline communist leadership were apparent. To hide their losing economic war against the South, they dwelled on the communists' usual tactics-propaganda, lying, and diversion. One of the diversionary strategies communists used was to send spies and a fifth column to infiltrate all branches of the democratic southern government and organize anti-government organizations, unions and even a court system. Kim Il-sung and his cronies had been using inhumane and evil power and methods to continue family succession of private religion of communism, murder, imprisonment and starving to their own people and to the brethren of South Koreans.

Facing the dangerous situation, President Park mobilized able bodies to work and fight, and eventually won the economic war against North Korea as a strong base for a peaceful unification. The army, navy and air force veterans came out to organize defense units village by village with access to guns and small arms to defend the village from infiltrated spies and their agents. Park's survival instinct worked and no major national security breach came to surprise the nation except the communist commando infiltration through the DMZ. It came within a few blocks of the Blue House, the executive office in Seoul. All were killed except two including Kim Sin-jo out of 31 men highly trained commandos with the specific purpose of assassinating Park Chung-hee in the Blue House. The survivor Kim, who had been adamant about his commando's mission to cut Park Chung-hee's neck, experienced a remarkable transformation, becoming a Christian minister. The mobilization also helped to revitalize the economic development with more efficient and organized workers from the villages.

At a designated time, people and cars on the streets stopped in attention for unity and patriotism, facing the national flag of Korea or the National Assembly building for the elected legislators. Park's single-handed effort to gather all forces and mobilize people in a large scale, military fashion opened up a new era for collective activity. Soon a national movement called Saemaul Undong and systematic industrialization were to begin. Both the national efforts required seed money and modern management systems to gather trained people for specific manufacturing/exporting activities and self-help to improve their villages.

In many instances in his life, Park showed remarkable survival instincts in pressure situations. Once, he worked at Munkyung

Elementary School as a young teacher after graduating from the teachers' school in Daegu. He inadvertently came into direct conflict with the Colonial School authority. The incident was about the colonial order to cut hair short. Park, the young teacher, had a little bit longer hair but was not willing to comply with the haircut order, thinking the order petty and nebulous. The school district superintendent came to the school and chided Park at the open dinner meeting welcoming the superintendent. Park exploded with highly emotional contempt disturbing the dinner party at the shock of the school principal, Park's boss, and those at the dinner table.

Soon after that episode, Park considered changing his career. He looked into a military position as his survival instincts directed him to be close to the power source of the nation and the military was a symbol of power. Becoming an officer in the Imperial Japanese Army would be a good solution to avoid continuing to listen to the belittling and contemptuous words *Joseanjing*, spoken in hushed tones by the local police and colonial officials. Park changed his career and became an officer whom the local officials would not dare call the Japanese "N" word within hearing distance of Park.

In another time of life and death situation after the unconditional surrender of Japan to the U.S. and allied forces, Park was arrested and being transported to Russian territory by the Russian army. He marshaled a daring escape from the convoy train with the help of Colonel Kim Dong-suk to escape sure death. He returned to his home village in the southern part of a poor farming town in worn-out army fatigues for the next phase of his life, fully apprehensive and vaguely hopeful. He desired to do something important and significant for the country finally independent and out of colonial shackles.

Korea had independence as a result of Japan's surrender and Korea was not a major participant in armed fighting along with the U.S. forces in the Pacific. Even though Korean partisans fought against Japanese forces along its northern border with Manchuria and Russia, Korea did not have much say about the U.S.-U.S.S.R. agreement to divide Korea along the 38th parallel. Russia occupied north of the 38th parallel without any fighting. In contrast, the U.S. moved into the south after many brutal battles in the Pacific. The division immediately brought enormous confusion and national disaster for Koreans desiring a unified nation with the same race, same culture, same language and even same types of food. The extreme confrontation between two diabolical ideologies, the first cold war front between democracy and communism, caused violent demonstrations, lynching of the opposite, plots, assassination and utter confusion, adding anarchy and lawless disorder.

The communist Kim Il-sung, hand picked and groomed by Stalin, had Stalin's full support to establish a Soviet satellite regime in the north. Kim Il-sung had an easier control of the North as his henchman had been working with Soviet military advisors with clockwork efficiency with Soviet troops ready to crush any resistance. Kim Il-sung's ambition did not stop there. Kim had already put communist agents in the South in turmoil to work with underground communist cells. These communists organized the South Labor Party right after independence in 1945. Park became a recruitment target of the communist underground party to use his military training and connections to infiltrate the South Korean army being organized. In ideological confusion and brother Sang-hee's influence, Park joined the underground communist party in 1945. The next year Park's brother Sang-hee was killed in the communist-organized demonstration by the South Korean police constabulary. The underground communist party did not lose time to manipulate Park, who joined the South Korean army to infiltrate the army with the conspicuous title, *Kunsa Chongchaek*, chief military commissar.

Park did not expect that his involvement with the underground party would become a life-and-death event for him when a South Korean army battalion assigned to put down communist rebellion in Cheju Island rebelled against the South Korean government. Soon Park's communist connection was investigated. He was found guilty and given a death sentence. Again Park had survival instincts placing himself close to the power source. Park was the chief of staff to General Paik Sun-yup, the supreme commander to put down the army rebellion. Luckily, Park was not clearly implicated with the rebellion in an active role or obvious subversive communist action except that he had an impressive communist title. As soon as he returned to his hometown after the surrender of Japan, the intelligent Park was watching and analyzing the two ideologies for their merit to help the poverty-stricken and chaotic country with foreign occupancy of the land. Park realized the two ideologies were put before Korea without their asking for it.

With confusion and lack of experience of the two ideologies in Korea, it was not easy to make a quick choice and Park's involvement in the political ideologies was superficial in the beginning of his career in South Korea. Again, Park's survival instincts dictated nothing but full cooperation in the serious investigation of communist cells in the army. Park turned over the complete organization chart of communist cells in the army. Park's close relationship with General Paik Sun-yup and Park's absence of clear and damaging communist activity convinced General Paik to recommend commutation of the death sentence to President Syngman Rhee. The death sentence was commuted to termination from his active position in the army. Park was saved miraculously.

Another time he displayed excellent survival instincts was with what he did after being fired from his position in the army. Most people might have uttered in the similar situation, "I have had enough." Not Park. His survival instincts told him, " It is better for a fish to stay in water no matter how shallow or dirty." Park stayed in the army, even though his position was an unpaid volunteer civilian assistant in the army intelligence section. Park's decision was precise as he had something productive to do without self-doubt or a feeling of guilt. Park knew from his life experience that it is a very tight corner where the waves turn. The strong wave that pushed Park mercilessly turned at that very tight corner when he met young graduates from the Korea Military Academy. These young army lieutenants had fresh enthusiasm to serve as army officers and courage to change the direction of the nation from the colonial *Yupjun Euisik*, the second class mentality, to a "we can do" military spirit. It was a perfect match between the young army lieutenants and the middle-aged civilian helper.

At that very corner, Park even met a matchmaker. Park had a chance to fulfill his conjugal happiness in having a respectable family, long after his first unwanted and sad marriage at a pre-puberty age arranged by his parents.

The Korean War lasted three years and one month and it was one of the most savage civil wars. It ignited the deadly confrontation of two political ideologies that skipped over basic human decency and family affection. Brothers murdered brothers, sons degraded fathers, and students assaulted teachers. The problem was the confrontation of democracy and communism, and Korea was on a collision course not because of its faults. The Korean Peninsula became a testing ground for modern weapons and even human waves from communist China as a war strategy. The war casualty was enormous, close to 4 million military and civilians of two Koreas and their allies. Park served as a major when the war called him back to active service where his military training and leadership were desperately needed. He was promoted to lieutenant colonel in September 1950 when the war reversed to push back the communists. Another rapid promotion followed to colonel in April 1951 and Park had risen to brigadier general by the time the Korean War ended with an armistice in July 1953. Park continued to rise in the military hierarchy to become a major general in 1958.

In a way, the Korean War saved him from the bottom and gave him a new opportunity. He served brilliantly during the war as an intelligence officer, artillery unit commander, division chief-of-staff and even division commander with rapid promotions during wartime service. Park used his military training, character strength, and his alumni ties of three military academies to become an effective military leader. Junior officers respected him for his uncommon honesty and charisma in dealing with problems and people in his military career. Park, seeing the country in ruins as if in the stone age and in perpetual poverty, was fascinated with the stories he read about a group of young military officers who changed the direction of Japan for rapid development and economic prosperity.

Park was a revolutionary in his mind as soon as he saw his country in bondage as a colonized nation under the brutal rule of Imperial Japan. Park's critical attitude toward corrupted politicians, especially during the third-term Syngman Rhee's first Republic, found him and his collaborating young army officers in a revolutionary plot to oust Syngman Rhee and corrupted politicians. Again, Park's survival instincts were on fine display in organizing and setting off the first armed revolution. Park and the team set the date at May 8, 1960 for the planned revolution to take over the corrupt government. When the tired people saw the corruption, injustice and ineffective economic policy, the majority of people wanted a drastic move like a revolution to happen and the general atmosphere was quite conducive to a military revolution.

Also within the military, the honest officers and soldiers witnessed the wanton corruption of the ruling liberal party and their cronies. Corrupt politicians and government officials took bribes, rigged elections, used gangs for political purposes, and created the lawless culture of high- class people with money and connections. The military revolution committee concluded it was time for action. A secret military plan called The 5.8 Plan was in the planning stages for quite some time to launch a coup after the planned general election scheduled on March 15th, 1960. The date for the coup was set for May 8, 1960, under looming controversy over the vice-presidency of Lee Ki-boog, a long-time associate of President Syngman Rhee. The election of Syngman Rhee was not in question because the opponent candidate died before the election, yet people had a big question as to whether Rhee was used at his senior age of 85 by corrupted liberty party members to continue the blood-sucking corruption.

The date of the coup by the military was set purposely on May 8th, 1960, as the army chief-of-staff general Song Yo-chan was scheduled to visit Washington D.C. on that date. Park's survival instincts prevailed to avoid General Song for the planned action as General Song was strictly loyal to president Rhee with deep respect. A forceful anti-coup action would be a possibility if President Rhee ordered Song to take that action. Bloody confrontation between the coup and royal forces was a possibility. Park tried to avoid that chance which became a moot question when the student uprising came by surprise on April 19, 1960. The military coup was unnecessary and Park's survival instincts played a role, not his crude impulses.

A year later, the bloodless 5.16 military Revolution finally took place like clockwork without creating a bloody civil war situation. Again, Park's brilliant survival instincts were on display when he involved the army chief of staff, Chang Do-yong, in secret and also somewhat openly for show to other skeptics. This action, implicating General Chang as a part of the revolution, clearly created enormous confusion for the government in power to take any forceful anti-revolutionary military action. The willful confusion created was classic and smart because many questions were raised regarding the impending revolution without quick definite answers. This helped to delay the dispatch of any anti-revolution force to quell the revolution in time. Questions in the military channels and government executive offices were: Is General Chang a part of the revolution? Has the revolution the full support of the army or not? What is happening? Is this a military revolution or some sort of security action? More simple but relevant questions were raised openly or in secret without prompt plausible answers. Even the military intelligence units were in limbo without knowing what to do.

General Chang was finally involved as the head of the revolution and many critical messages to the nation including the pledge of the revolution went out in Chang's name, consolidating the impression of full army support and people's approval of the action. However, within two months of the revolution in place, General Chang was arrested on charges of being an anti-revolutionary. Park and the revolutionary team had the genius to use confusion as a cover for the revolution to succeed until the very last minute.

The mindset for survival was everywhere in Park's demeanors and habits, especially in pressure situations. Two days before the launch of the 5.16 Revolution, Park's confidante, Kim Jong-pil, came to Park with an urgent problem. Kim reported that the planned revolution was leaked when the police unit under the prime minister Chang Myun arrested a key revolutionary member. It would only be a matter of time before there would be full disclosure of the revolutionary plan. Kim asked in a troubled voice, " What shall we do?" Without hesitation, Park's simple and terse response was, " Proceed as planned!" Park's quick reasoning came from his survival instincts. He asked himself, "Can the coup member arrested and being interrogated withstand two days with a tight lip?" Park quickly added, "If the revolution is any good, God will give us two days." Park also worried and repeated his earlier remarks concerning the danger of a coup, "If the revolution succeeds, we will be the government force, if it loses we will become the rebel enemy." "Push the plan as it is" was the marching order. In that short sentence, wisdom for and confidence in survival found their course to follow. Nothing happened to kill the coup plan, and the revolution went on full speed.

During his eighteen years of leadership in government, making rapid changes for economic revolution, many more crises came to Park and a few life-and-death incidents. Also, a few political suicides like North Korea's assassination commando attack known as Kim Sin-jo happened in 1968 and political upheavals occurred to oust him from power. In 1974, at the Korea Independence Day ceremony,

Park's wife, the first lady, was gunned down by Moon Se-kwang, a Korean resident in Japan living in democratic freedom but belonging to *Jochongryun,* a communist association of Koreans in Japan. At every time of crisis, Park showed remarkable restraint and survival instincts with or without the intervention of providence. Moon, the assassin, first aimed his gun at Park but missed because of the blinding reflection of light from the platform. The stray bullet hit the First Lady Yuk Young-soo, who was sitting on the platform, in the head. Park continued the Independence Day speech behind the podium as if all was in order, although the first lady was being rushed out for emergency medical treatment. After Park finished his speech and the function was concluded, he walked calmly to the first lady's seat to recover a small handbag and inexpensive Korean-style rubber shoes. A calm and collected demeanor was Park's hallmark survival instinct during times of crisis.

During his presidency, Park launched many mammoth-scale projects to usher in the new era of long-awaited economic development and industrialization. The projects were ambitious in the small country without natural resources on a scale and with a speed never seen in many millenniums. The purpose of all these projects was to achieve economic revolution that must proceed to bring in a real democratic revolution. When Park pushed all feasible national projects affecting his government's survival, he applied his remarkable survival instincts to complete the project. When the Gyeongbu (Seoul-Busan) Expressway, the first superhighway project in Korea patterned after West Germany's super highway construction, took off with high hopes, the opposition parties in Korea vehemently opposed the project. The opposition leaders equated the project to wealthy golfers' easy access to golf courses at the expense of poor farmers cultivating the land. The opposition of the project was vociferous and extreme. For instance, the opposition political leaders showed their dramatic denial of the project by lying down on the dirt in front of the bulldozers hard at work to shorten the construction time of the difficult project.

Gyeongbu Expressway was the biggest and most expensive civil engineering project in Korea in its 5,000 year history. It presented the biggest challenge to Park's government as bulldozers were just one step behind the engineers with the blueprints of the design in their hands to adjust for the field construction conditions. Very often the engineers doing the design worked with the construction crew with bulldozers following. This was President Park Chung-hee's ultimatum to the war of modernization. Park and government officials regarded the project as the main harbinger of the nation's economic development. President Park focused on the construction of the superhighway as his marching orders to follow.

In his Blue House office, he hung a working-scale map of 1:250,000 for his input to the design and construction progress as the bright hope for the long-awaited economic development. Difficult loans from West Germany and hard-negotiated compensation from Japan were applied to the project. The completion of the project was so important as to give the project the highest priority in funding and construction follow-up. President Park was involved in every phase of the project as if he were the project manager and the construction superintendent. Many nights, the construction company heads slept on the construction site to expedite the construction progress and to meet the president visiting the site in the dawn hours with the project blueprints in hand.

Park provided his input even to the right-of-way matters of the alignment of the superhighway, advising design engineers not to allow any structures within so many meters from the highway shoulder line for possible future widening of the superhighway when traffic increased. Park devoted all his waking life, day and night, solely to the completion of the epoch-making event . Park's survival instincts worked well and the project, a 428 km superhighway, was completed in the shortest time and at the lowest cost when compared with similar projects around the world. The successful completion of the superproject at long last opened the age of Korea's industrialization and the resulting elimination of the chronic poverty for the first time in Korean history.

President Park was instrumental in assembling people, money, and forces to support the revolutionary agenda in all aspects of national reconstruction and modernization. Obviously, Park's survival instinct played a role in his life events and in his revolutionary work with a hand-picked team in the fulfillment and maintenance of his life goals. The historical achievement of the Miracle of the Han River was possible because of him and the forces he gathered around him. Integration of causes and events came to a fruitful and successful conclusion because of visible intentions and the perseverance of Park and his followers.

Nevertheless, all was not in their control. Knowingly or unknowingly, many other forces were at work. Providence is the only way to explain the successful course of his life and the revolutionary goals. For instance, the revolution took its own course by chance. The revolutionary force of about 3,600 men out of a 600,000-man army was not a guarantee for the bloodless and successful conclusion of revolution. Direct orders from any of the national and the Joint Military command of the U.S. and Republic of Korea did not come to crush the revolution when launched. The 1st Army did not mobilize any forces to oppose the revolution even though the supreme commander of the 1st Army was Lee Han-rim, who opposed the revolution in principle. The leadership in Washington, President Kennedy and the Secretary of State, Dean Rusk, were away visiting Canada. An unexpected parade of Korea Military Academy cadets came in support of the revolution at a very critical moment. Many other unplanned and uncontrollable forces were added without human explanation but possible as the work of providence. The old adage, "man proposes, god disposes" may fit the circumstances surrounding Park and his national agenda for industrialization and liberation from poverty.

3

LEADERS

"Follow me!"

"Follow me!" was a distinct command that Park was acquainted with early in life through military training and throughout his continuous service in the military. Park lived with this command all his life, first as a cadet of Manchukuo Imperial Military Academy, then the Japanese Army Academy, Korea Military Academy and finally as the revolutionary leader and the president. The Korea Military Academy was established in a hurry under the U.S. Army Military Government in Korea (USAMGIK) to maintain security and order during the chaotic period from liberation to the forming of the Republic of Korea. During the fratricidal Korean War started by communist North Korea with massive Soviet-made tanks and weaponry, Park led army units for intelligence- gathering and combat duties. He watched gallant young officers with lieutenant insignia on their shoulders wearing their helmets with the written commands on the back leading their platoons to the enemy line. War is brutal and unfair, especially to the weaker side. Yet, Park was in awe seeing lieutenants in their early twenties leading their platoons to the baptism of bullets as if they had a divine shield around them. He was a lieutenant himself in the Manchukuo Army just before Japan's unconditional surrender. Freedom is not free and his thoughts raced back to his childhood and growing years searching for real leaders in his life who formed who and what he was.

Among leaders, Park's first and foremost leader in his boyhood was his mother. Though reluctant at first, once the baby was born, the mother was all about devotion and love to give the youngest son the feeling of security and safety in the best way she knew how. She had many children to raise already, two girls and four boys, in a poor declining scholar family with limited resources and money. Korea at the time was in a dire condition, especially the farming region in the southern part of the country under Japanese colonial rule. Japanese colonial policy to use Korea as their logistics center for their expansion to the Asian continent emphasized the industrialization of the northern part of Korea for mining resources and farming in the south because of good weather, especially, farming of rice to supply to their burgeoning army. Rice was essential for the Japanese army and considered as a gift from the emperor. Much of rice produced in the region went to the battlefronts, thereby causing the starvation of native Korean farmers and their families. Members in poor families, especially those too young or too old to work, had a tough time getting enough food, even after their harvest.

In this hand-to-mouth living, the mother paid special attention to feeding her son with nutritious food, but always her means were so limited. The mother felt pain when there was not enough food on the table for growing children with large appetites. Meat was almost non-existent except on special family days or traditional holidays to remember ancestors whose function was heavily influenced by Confucian teaching. Mother gathered edible foodstuffs to prepare meals such as grains, fruits, vegetables, herbs, roots, occasional chickens, eggs and even snails painstakingly dug up from water-soaked rice paddies.

Mother's heart sank when food was not enough. She saved food items, especially rice, so that she could make a humble lunchbox the next morning for her youngest son to take to his school miles away on foot. When morning came, the mother was happy to prepare a meager lunchbox with the saved rice mixed with barley or other cheaper grains with seasoned vegetable or dried radish and rarely a small portion of scrambled eggs with shrimp sauce. Mother wrapped the lunch box with thin square cloths tied at four corners for her son to carry securely apart from other school items. The lunchbox so prepared was very meager in substance but so rich with mom's love, trust and big dreams for her son.

Every morning the mother had the joy of seeing her youngest son going off to school on foot. She usually came out of the house with her son to the narrow dirt road leading to the main macadam road where people walked to the school and town government offices. After a deep bow, the mother stood on the road watching her son walking fast and briskly toward school. She usually stood on the road corner until the son was barely visible. Now, the son gone, the mother walked back to her busy morning chores. The mother was happy to see her son, though small, was healthy and booksmart. The son liked to learn interesting subjects such as mathematics, geology, and history. The son was happy to see his mother waving her small hands for quite some time to give him the mother's love and confidence for son's success in school and beyond. Daily, mother and son had their own time to share their burden of extreme poverty and the helpless feeling of living as colonized people.

In these conditions of a large family in poverty, in brutal colonial oppression, and in helplessness about the future, the mother and her youngest son stuck together to find normalcy and security for the large family with brothers, sisters and parents living under one roof. Very active but slender and small the son was, yet he was adjusting well at school. Also he did well on schoolwork without much help from family members. Quiet and self-reliant for his age, her son became her pride and the hope of the family. The smiling face and the encouraging words from the mother were strong motivation for the son to try his best in whatever task he had in class. Mother always showed supreme devotion to the family and was ready to sacrifice anything for the growing children, especially the youngest. Her attitude gave her son emotional stability, mental strength and the self-image of "can-do" early in life.

After a full day of separate work, one at school, the other at a small but cozy and clean mud house, a joyful reunion came when the tired-looking but briskly-walking son with a tiny school bag approached the waiting mother who stood at the same spot as in the morning. The mother was there as if she had stood there all day. The son's walking grew faster when he saw the mother waving her hands and smiling at a distance. The son was glad to see his mother's unmistakable sign of welcome and approval of his learning at school that day. The mother's smile and hug when they touched each other were all the son needed to complete the school day with a sense of success and accomplishment.

The mother's feeling was mutual and she gave a deep breath of relief for the day, believing the day was over safely. The mother felt guilty about not wanting the baby early on in her pregnancy at the age of 45. Her guilt made her give more attention to the youngest son as if she needed forgiveness from her son. The fragile body and dark complexion of her son was a constant reminder for the mother to give him emotional and mental strength however possible. The son's adjustment in school and his smart and strong behavior gave the mother extra joy. The mother and son's daily ritual continued as the son grew and the large poor family somehow managed itself without major crisis. The household continually paid special attention to the children's education when the youngest was developing a special kinship with one of his older and smart brothers Sang-hee. The older brother Sang-hee slowly filled the position of a mentor and a role model as they grew up together and the mother prematurely became old and weak because of the strain and the pressure of keeping the poor large family fed and nourished.

At Gumi Elementary School in North Gyeongsang Province, Park was doing well scholastically in logic and comprehension subjects such as mathematics, history, and geography. He was superior to other classmates even in reasoning subjects such as sociology and philosophy. Overall, he was a good student with teachers' approval and classmates' recognition. Paradoxically, though, classmates and the teachers called him "little black boy" for his physical appearance. Park was a bit introverted, quiet, and shy. Yet every year, he was class president, not because of his outgoing leadership but because of his scholastic merit in the class. In the Japanese system of education at the time, the class president was not elected by classmates but was appointed by the teacher based on scholastic achievement. Park was the number-one student so he became class president. The position of class president gave him enormous self-confidence and a robust self-image despite the degrading nickname of "little black boy" and he did not care how he looked but dreamed what big things he could accomplish later in life.

Luckily, he was not the first son in the family to worry about the family's sustenance and future wellbeing. As the youngest of seven children, he had the freedom and luxury to daydream about life, about the colonized country he lived in, and the world. He started to read voraciously whatever books he could get his hands on, especially books on heroes: Napoleon, Alexander the Great, Plutarch, Emperor Meiji of Japan, famous military commanders in Korea, Yi Soon-sin, King Sejong and other kings in Korean history, American revolutionary leaders and Abraham Lincoln. However, the Korean history books were hard to get as Japanese colonial policy to eradicate Korean history was in effect at the time. The Japanese policy was to integrate Korea for the bigger Rising Sun in Asia. Park, as the last-born child, had a disproportionate amount of love, attention, and encouragement from the family, especially from his mother, the essential ingredients of self-assured military leaders and national heroes. With these ingredients and the call of duty, Park became a revolutionary hero transforming the poorest country in the world to a world power of democracy. He built a foundation for peaceful unification of Korea by democrats and democratic principles and not by communism and Kim Il-sung's family cult.

More leaders, real or imaginary, showed up in Park's conscious mind as he pursued schooling and read many books on military or political heroes he wanted to emulate. He was, now, learning quickly as an intelligent and sensitive young man. He started questioning deep inside of him why Koreans were subject to Japanese colonial rule and what brought his beloved country to the state of colonization and brutal oppression. Through his reading, he came to know many brave leaders in the world. Yet, he knew that his true leader was not one of those remarkable people but his own mother who gave him emotional stability, inner strength and moral character to lead people and not just take orders. He knew he had many handicaps but he had to think big if he wanted to live up to his mother's expectations. Young as he was, he was ready to tackle the tough courses before him for his future.

4

IMPOVERISHED BY MONARCHS

"We have to innovate on the present condition of society and politics."

"Does smoke come out of the chimney without the fireplace burning?" is an old Korean aphorism regarding causes and effects of life events. Many people living under Japan's colonial occupation asked the same question over and over again about why Korea was in that lamentable colonized situation. Even after liberation in 1945, more educated people asked the same question when they faced the chaos and anarchy caused by the division of the country into two diametrically different regimes, one communist and the other democratic. Park Chung-hee was no exception and often thought the burning fireplaces of Korea to consider were three: monarchs, colonists and communists. They were the cause of the demise of Korea. To improve social, political and economic conditions in Korea, the first thing to do was the honest study of the three burning fireplaces, Park thought.

The monarchic government was the dominant form of rule on the Korean peninsula from generation to generation. The last Yi dynasty was more than 500 years old, maintaining an independent nation in a precarious geographic situation among bigger and stronger countries surrounding it, mainly China, Russia, and Japan. The monarch was always in conflict when the political and military equilibrium was absent among these surrounding countries.

In Korea, as in other parts of the world where republicanism was neither known nor imagined, the form of government had been monarchic rule. The kings in Korea occupying their throne had the absolute power to rule during the Yi dynasty, named after its Yi Tae Jo well over 500 years ago. A monarch was the center of power, usually occupied a throne and represented the rule of a person, half god and half man. Monarchic rule is the opposite of republicanism where the power comes from the consent of people being governed.

Korea has been historically unstable because of its geography with three sides to the ocean and one side with access to the vast Asian continent. The direct access created problems because it served as a bridge for powerful and bigger countries surrounding the Korean peninsula, notably the empires of China, Russia and Japan. When the equilibrium vanished, a political vacuum appeared, attracting various strong neighboring countries and making Korea a battlefield and its innocent people victims of war. Death, maiming and painful psychological disfigurement were the outcome of the conflicts unavoidable by Korea, the host country. Furthermore, this instability and potential disaster made the monarch and the people pursue an easy way out. They tried to second-guess the potential winner of the conflict and align with the winner beforehand. When the guess was right, there was a less painful outcome of the conflict, and if the guess was wrong, catastrophe followed.

Consequently, people looked for a powerful centralized government and they did not mind clinging to the hierarchy with rigid social classes which made people of the lower class live with a bleak outlook continuously, living in austere poverty without knowing where the next meal was coming from. Moreover, the government tried to align with outside forces for the country's defense rather than embarking on the tough tasks of restoring the country. The ancient military and economic system failed to meet the basic needs of the people for food and national security. In addition, the founding monarch of the Joseon dynasty, Yi Tae Jo, adopted Confucian philosophy as a guiding policy of social, economic and political governance. He consolidated the nation after its successful military coup against the previous Goryeo Dynasty which had more than 470 years of nationhood following Buddhism as its political and social precept. Yi Tae Jo wanted to compensate for the drawbacks of Buddhism by changing to Confucian philosophy as the ruling strategy. Confucianism is a moral and political guide based on Chinese tradition and beliefs with emphasis on family loyalty, ancestor worship, and wives' respect for husbands, among other practical teachings. It is a morality rather than a religion. Confucianism and its tradition was a convenient tool for monarchs of the Joseon Dynasty for ruling people with emphasis on ethics and behavior.

Nevertheless, Confucian ideas had major defects as time went on and was blamed for its negative influence on people with long-term social effects. The negative influence of Confucian philosophy came out over a long period of practice, first imperceptibly with the feeling of good more than bad but after a few generations of uninspiring monarchs' reign, their influence became formidable, affecting all segments of people's lives. The bad influence of Confucian traditions came cheaply because of its rigidity and formality of the philosophy. They tended to close people's minds and also stop the ruling class's willingness to change ineffective policies, rules and regulations. The keeping of "the status quo" became the main concern of everyone, especially those in power that had authority, and they refused modernization of government policy, social reforms and the military apparatus for the defense of the country.

As the Industrial Revolution with the invention of the steam engine started to free mankind from manual labor and physical exertion, it also broadened military technology and means of transport to such a magnitude that modernization became essential to compete with other nations in commerce and military matters. Defense of the country depended more and more on modernization of weapons and troop organization. Arrow and shield battle approach was no longer valid but the monarchs closed their minds and did not pay attention beyond the local tribal matters with strong family ties. There, the overall interests tended to be clannish, self-justifying and fact-bending manipulations jeopardizing the country's independence and progress. The absolute power of the monarchs was either absolute good or absolute bad depending on who was on the throne. Luckily, the common wisdom that says 20% of good leaders makes up 80% of good results applied to the Joseon Dynasty.

A few good monarchs did outstanding work to make the kingdom organized, guided and strengthened to maintain the nation's independence and cultural tradition for five hundred years. Already, outside of the Korean monarchy, an unprecedented political enlightenment by landlords and noblemen had started on the opposite side of the world in England. The revolutionary idea of Magna Carta, the Great Charter, to limit the absolute power of the monarchs had come about for the protection and guarantee of the rights of citizens many centuries earlier in 1215. The revolutionary idea of Magna Carta was not known and it did not have any impact on the sleepy kingdom of the Joseon Dynasty which was clinging to the oldest political institution, the monarchy.

Park Chung-hee was a diligent student of history and soon after his elementary education, he paid more time and effort to learn about the victory and defeat of countries with his uncanny analytical attitude, first by reading Chinese history of both formal publications and informal folklore. Park learned about the decline of Korean monarchs that continued on the small Korean peninsula despite a few great monarchs' effort and accomplishments. The succession of power was by heritage only and as the succession was further down in generations from the first revolutionary idea and momentum, the monarchs and people were subject to the passive teaching of Confucian philosophy and its guiding rules. As a consequence, the dynasty further lost the enthusiasm for reform and revitalization of the people and the country, resulting in a humdrum existence and status quo.

Many defeatist and self-defeating behaviors and idiosyncrasies started in a pervasive manner. Division of people was pervasive by rigid social class, regions, education, marriage and work, plus whatever criteria that gives one party advantage over another party, whether material or emotional. Undoubtedly, the human instinct to kill and conquer was on clear display even though it was subtle and passive because of Confucian teaching and its emphasis on moderation or the middle of the road. Not hot, not cold, just lukewarm but enough to boil people's hearts to wish to overthrow the governing system and the class structure which the ruling class and the monarch wanted to keep. Later in history, not-too-distant from the present moment, during the Cultural Revolution in Red China, the young zealots of the cultural revolution that Chairman Mao sanctioned, frequently attacked Confucian traditions and government leaders following the old principles with public shame and even torture.

In Korea, according to the Cultural Revolution, people under monarchs with Confucian adherence were passive, divisive, maligned laborers who adored foreign powers and were reluctant to change the sorry state of national and personal affairs, in short not fitting for revolutionary work. Appenzeller, an ambitious and devoted missionary from America, came to Korea during the turn of the century and was dismayed to see people lazy, hating work, dangerously factional and ignorant of what was going on in the world.

Park's family was poor and large to feed and to educate. Park was to give up after elementary education because of the poverty in a brutally colonized country in the farming region of the southern part of Korea without industry and commerce. Park's older brother Sang-hee, his mentor and unabashed leader, urged Park Chung-hee to pursue an educational career as their farming and the poverty of the family did not provide an alternative. The brother's friendly, yet strong advice worked and Park went on to take a tough entrance examination for the coveted teachers' colleges. The Japanese colonial government funded teachers' schools with great mission and with full support of the imperial monarch in Tokyo, Japan. The central government had the strength and power gained from modernization and ambitious restoration by the Meiji Revolutionary Council. Japan had a big and ambitious plan to colonize the great Asia and Pacific basin.

The colonial government established three teachers' schools, in Pyongyang, Seoul, and Daegu on the Korean peninsula. The three teachers' schools were for three regions of Korea: north, central, and south, and Daegu was not far from Park's home. The competition to enroll was stiff with a ratio of more than ten applicants to every one chosen. Education was offered tuition-free. Room and board, and the yearly school trip were an individual responsibility, applying enormous pressure to Park for the necessary money. Besides, employment after graduation was guaranteed. Park passed the examination and enrolled in the school with an examination rank of 51 out of 100 for the five-year program. Nevertheless, the feeling of success was short-lived as Park entered the elite group of students and the best teaching staff the Imperial Government authority could assemble for the big picture of Japanese domination and ruling of the Pacific-Indian Ocean region and subarea.

Parks' enthusiasm for study at the five-year elite teachers' school did not last as he was sensitive and judgmental about the situation of Korea in the colonized land where the total integration of Korean culture, people, and the territory with Imperial Japan was in rapid progress. He just wanted to get by, believing that he could complete the teacher's school without too much problem if he concentrated a little bit. Yet, he realized that the government-sponsored education was to develop teachers for Japan's bright future as the dominant master colonizing the country by obliterating Korean history and tradition. The realization saddened Park and other sensitive Korean students as they were born in the depths of Japanese colonial brutality and knew how it was to be without their own country. Park's protracted absence from school work did not help his scholastic achievement either as he had to scramble for funds for his dormitory expense by taking time off.

On top of this gloomy atmosphere for the young and intelligent students, heart wrenching emotional pain came as if adding salt to the wound for many students from Confucian-impacted families. At the young age of 18, Park had to go through a family-arranged wedding in 1936 to a 16-year-old young girl named Kim Ho Nam even before he completed teachers' school. Park was convinced he had other important things to learn and to accomplish before having a wife and family that might bind him. Marriage at a very young age was common because of the long influence of Confucian practice and family desire to insure the workforce in the predominant farming community. Nevertheless, the early marriage practice exerted innumerable pressures and unwanted relationships that robbed young people's ambition and adventures in political, scientific and other challenging fields. As a result, a spirit of exploration and invention was replaced with a passive and safety-first lifestyle to protect family concerns. Also the closed-mind attitude towards changes and revolutionary ideas tended to make impotent individuals, groups and the nation slowly and definitely.

In 1937 Park graduated from the teachers' school at the bottom of the class with the class rank of 69 out of 70 students showing his true nature of exploring something bigger and more exciting than the traditionally safe and mediocre job of a teacher. Nevertheless, while at the teachers' school with sensitive and ambitious young men, and before jumping into a career position as an elementary school teacher at the forefront of Japanese colonization, Park had ample time and energy to look back in history. He studied about the demoralizing impact of the monarchical rule on the Korean peninsula for the last 500 years.

Even though about 20% of good kings created effective national policies and rules for the kingdom's culture, inventions and communal spirit, in the overall scheme of things, that was not enough to compete in the harsh world of international conflicts among nations. The 80% weak or outright bad kings caused further division of people, class hatred, lethargy, and inadequate military power for self-defense. Concerns for ruling came first before any effort to build community, depriving the kingdom of the chance to unite and collectively improve the quality of life and defense of the nation.

Throughout the Joseon Dynasty, succession of power was problematic when weak kings involved as powerful people at the periphery came to the very front of succession adding oil to the fire. Factions, relatives, and extended families were quickly mobilized to purge, kill, and force exile upon whomever was in the way of them grabbing succession and power. Years, even generations, of the practice to divide and form factions for survival did not give wisdom to the ruling class to search for a mutually beneficial ground for all to survive and prosper. Extreme measures arose from the use of private armies, assassins, and influence from powerful people such as former king's consorts and in-laws to destroy each other rather than building consensus for the social, economic, and political unity, and the economic and military strength of the nation.

The presence of 40 – 50% slave population in the country under the control of royal families and upper-class people, in mid-18th century Korea, with a total population of 19 million and with the life expectancy of 24 years for male and 26 years for female, indicated the difficult living conditions. As a result, the kingdom became a Hermit Kingdom afraid of opening its doors to the western and more developed nations. The hopeless nation and its people saw so much strife of princesses, martyred ministers supporting right succession of power, and incessant divisions of ruling class losing sight of people's welfare and nation's defense, but narrowly focused only on their power and wealth.

The helpless nation witnessed, year in and year out, laughable divisions of government officials and power- hungry people into the Easterners and Westerners; then soon to Northerners and Southerners; then again into Noron and Soron. Bloody purges continued, at one time more than one thousand people were killed for a power shuttle from one group to another as in the case of Chung Yeo-Rip's conflict. Good policy like *HyangYak* was promulgated by King Jung-Jong to instill local autonomy and community self-help by using the leadership of the charismatic minister named Cho Kwang-Jo but the policy could not last long. Soon, differing factions didn't want to see Cho's popularity and his accumulation of power and did not hesitate to use any and all tricks and rumors to pull down Cho. Many opposing factions did all they could to corner and displace such wise and courageous government leaders like Cho Kwang Jo, a farsighted reformer during the mid-18th century Yi Dynasty.

No dirty tricks were off the table to those factions plotting the demise of their opponent faction in power or any sub groups threatening the plotting faction's strength and organization. Outrageous and dirty tactics were devised and applied to accuse and then incriminate the powerful reformers who spearheaded many required reforms with initial support from the king and other high government leaders. Yet, Cho's opponents did not like to see more power being gathered and channeled to Cho and his faction. Jealousy was boiling in their hearts and they started circulating rumors, first in secret then out in the open, to make their case stick.

The rumor was that Minister Cho was using the power he gathered to overturn the government and the king who was in a weaker position because rebelling ministers had installed him on the throne. Hard evidence of Cho's plot to overthrow the king did not exist. A cunning and crafty plan was devised to put honey on leaves for caterpillars to eat up and leave four legible letters that said, "Cho will be the next king." That scheme worked and it was taken as a message from the supernatural, and for the weak and insecure king, the implied message was like a hot knife cutting through butter. Soon, Cho was cornered with suspicion of revolt and he met his untimely death at the hands of executioners. His visionary reform work to narrow the gap between the rich and the poor as well as other modernizing measures were thrown out, causing the nation to zig zag towards a weaker and more corrupt state.

Park Chung-Hee learned the history of the Joseon Kingdom by heart. He detested politicians, ever divisive and corrupt to mislead kings and disturb the nation's path to prosperity and self-defense on account of a selfish family's and clan's power and wealth. The more Park read about the history of the monarchical Korean kingdom, the more he came to abhor politicians who did not care about honest analysis of current conditions of the country and any visionary plans for the nation.

The Confucian ideals of ownership or property and filial piety were not inferior guiding principles by themselves but ineffective interpretation and application made nation's leaders and people naive, passive, and factional. Eighteen ranks and grades in government bureaucracy and the use of different colored clothes according to rank further divided and separated people, and made unity of people and national goals the exception rather than the norm. Important government policies had a wide range of different interpretations and applications, causing them to sway national policies for one particular faction's benefit. People tended to mistrust what the government did and would do. Nevertheless, brilliant exceptions existed. For example, the Annals or *Sillok*, the record of the Joseon Dynasty, had an uninterrupted and conscientious application, making the record the longest in the world of its kind, recording 452 years of a single dynasty.

When the succession of the throne was in jeopardy and a weak king was on the seat, people with royal family ties, in-laws, consorts and other relatives came to have great power to steer the government operations and policies to capricious and chaotic situations, making the nation weak. On occasion, courageous reformers risked their lives to implement just and equitable policies to stop rampant slavery in the nation like the Kabo Reform in 1894. However, it was too little too late to change the fortune of the country and to avoid the shameful annexation by Japan later.

Japan, through the Meiji Restoration, opened the country and united to modernize the country with an honest assessment of its weak and unstable condition while the neighboring Korean kingdom closed their doors and remained a hermit kingdom losing valuable time and opportunities to modernize and build national strengths and self-defense.

Japan's well-coordinated and united effort continued and, in a mere twenty-some years, they were ready to colonize defenseless peoples like the Yi Dynasty. Yet Japan's colonization of the Korean kingdom was neither free nor easy to attain. Japan had the secret agreement with the U.S., known as the Katsura-Taft agreement, which stipulated that Japan and the U.S. would not interfere with each other's colonization objectives, Korea for Japan, and Philippine for the U.S. Even after the agreement, Japan had to go war with China and Russia and win before they could annex Korea without objection. The Korean king KoJong and the people had to accept the shameful loss of their country as the result of unworthy monarchism, failed national policies, and national divisions. When the Yi Dynasty opened in 1392, she had a brilliant motto, *Daemyung Cheonji*, meaning, "Let there be light on the land and in the heavens." Park's intensive but secret study of Korean history gave him a sad reality about the condition of his beloved country. He murmured, "the light stopped, for how long?"

Clearly, Park saw the unwanted bad influence of the failed marriage of Korean monarchs with Confucian philosophy. He saw with deep sadness in his heart the three main failures of Korean monarchic rule for the five centuries of a bygone era on the Korean peninsula as follows:

—Massive chronic poverty

—Narrow world view based on tribal and family interests

—Passive attitude clinging to the status quo

5

BRUTALIZED BY COLONIALISTS

"What did those little boys do wrong?"

Park was sensitive and smart to see the hopeless situation that people lived in in a colonized country where the new masters and their enforcers were threatening native Koreans with a variety of weapons ready to trample them down if people resisted. Pistols, rifles and Samurai swords were on constant display as a sign of a potential threat and oppression. Especially, the well-groomed and fast commandos on horse were used to elicit fear. They intimidated people as ruthless and brutal soldiers and policemen handling any resistance, violent or peaceful, without tolerance.

Exploitation was the first word that came to Park's conscious mind as he grew up mentally and emotionally at the elementary school with his mother's devotion and constant encouragement. His mother's devotion to her youngest son was complete. Park felt subtle hesitation and resistance in the classroom because Japanese history, culture, and language was a major part of the education they received. The feelings of inadequacy and an inferiority complex were pervasive wherever Koreans gathered and worked. Even at family gatherings, the sad feeling of losing their identity as Koreans and their independence as people with their own culture, tradition, and even favorite foods and popular songs spread with sighs and blank looks. Listening to family members, especially his older brother and mentor Sang-hee and his friends, who were secretly involved in the Korean independence movement, Park realized the reality of their precarious situation in Korea that faced the progressively brutal colonial government and the progress of WWII.

Already, more than two decades had passed since Japan

systematically colonized Korea according to the goals the ambitious nation planned to accomplish starting with the 1910 annexation. Japan wanted to be dominant in the Asia-Pacific region against European and American powers in the Atlantic Ocean and its seaboard. In 1932, after more than two decades of the Japanese rule of Korea, Park enrolled and started his career training at the Teachers' School under the Japanese educational policy to integrate Koreans into the Japanese mainstream to conduct the widening war effort for the bigger war against the formidable enemy, the United States. Japan wanted to integrate Korea in no uncertain terms as soon as possible, physically, socially, and culturally, so that the two countries might function as one nation with all efficiency and effectiveness to win the war.

Park's operational arena since he enrolled in the teacher's school expanded geographically and intellectually for the country boy Park. He had many discussions with his intellectual friends in a more conducive city environment. There, Koreans were concerned not only with the immediate Japanese colonial issues but also the Korean independence movements as they knew about the Provisional Korean Government established in Shanghai, China and its operation. Park's physical move from Gumi, a small village, to Daegu, a larger city, created a more vigorous and urgent atmosphere to study about colonialism and its disadvantageous effects on a smaller and weaker country like Korea surrounded by more powerful countries. Park learned quickly that colonialism had a long history starting in the 16th century for territorial expansion and exploitation of the indigenous population for labor and material supply for the benefit of the dominant country. He recognized the enormous unfairness and inequity of the relationship between the dominant and subordinate countries involving colonization. He came to know that sufficient power with national and political consequence was a must not to be a victim of colonization and his yearning for power left an indelible mark deep inside his mind but hidden for self-protection.

Many young Korean intellectuals living under Japanese colonial rule were educated by teachers whose main objective was to indoctrinate Korean students with Japanese interests. The irony for many Koreans was that they all had deep in their heart the simple question of "why?" Why did Korea become the colony of Japan? Why couldn't Koreans stand up and fight to escape this sorry reality of an annexed country of a neighboring country? What will happen to all Koreans? Will all be Japanese nationals and subjects of the Empire of Japan for good? Why and how did Japan became a dominant country? How did Japan develop the national strength and power? Koreans, especially young curious students with independence and justice on their minds, could not escape all these questions even though it had been more than two decades since the Japanese occupation of Korea. Many saw the futility of their questions after all this time gone by. Questions and discussions of could-have-been, should-have-been, and might-have-been were nothing but laments and useless what-if mental exercises. Regardless, young Koreans asked the questions repeatedly in their innocent hearts as they were trying to develop their own careers as best they could under Japanese law and Japanese rules and regulations dictated by their political system.

Park Chung-hee was smart and sensitive. Deep into the night after boring daily student's work, he started questioning and finding answers by learning both Korean and Japanese history. Park read about the recent modernization of Japan and its leaders who recognized the need for reform and its follow-through. Immediately, Park's attention was glued to Japanese history dealing with its modernization during the Emperor Meiji period. The name Meiji means "enlightened rule." The rapid, well-coordinated reformation and modernization in less than two decades tantalized the young Park with envy and curiosity. Park found that the Meiji Restoration, also called Revolution or Reform, started in 1868 when Japan was chaotically divided by social classes, warlords and geographic partitions.

He also realized with distinct clarity that Japan had long been under Confucian influence as Korea was with a rigid social hierarchy in the order of Scholars, Farmers, Craftsmen, and Merchants. Over 1.9 million Samurais displaying long swords on their side belonged to the first class Scholars wreaking havoc due to the financial burden their country had to bear to pay Samurais. How was the Meiji Restoration (Park thought it should be called Revolution for the massive impact on the nation) possible while the neighboring country, Korea, was in a deep sleep? Korea was in a terrible condition with social divisions by *Yangban* (noble class) and *Sang Nom* (lower class) along with vicious political infighting. The "how?" was a large question thrown at Park. Park had no escape from the question but to wrangle with it for a small hint.

Japan's modernization was spellbinding for its speed and integration of efforts, first controlling warlords and then exercising a comprehensive national all-out effort under the motto of "Enrich the nation, strengthen the army." What was the initiative for the Meiji Revolution? The initiative was that the ruling class had an honest understanding of conditions in Japan as lagging behind European and American powers. The threatening visit of American Commodore Matthew Perry in 1867 in big warships was more than a mere wake-up call. It was perceived as the marching order for change with honest recognition of fears of attack by the Western and European powers.

The enlightened rulers of Japan welcomed the visitor Perry and his party in their big ships with their modern weapons. They opened the door with courageous admission of weakness and inferiority. The situation in Korea was a stark contrast when foreign warships visited. Park knew from Korean history that Koreans had the same incidents of receiving threatening foreign visitors and their reaction was the complete opposite. A small party from the U.S. commanded by General Sherman came to Korea in 1866, and the Korean government failed to honestly assess their situation. Out of ignorance of world conditions, they attacked and killed the Westerners and the chance for reform evaporated for good and their modernization did not take place.

The two opposite ways of handling the condition of backwardness by the two adjacent countries, Japan and Korea, were night and day and, essentially, life and death. The difference in reaction ended up controlling the long future history of the two neighboring countries, one dominant and the other submissive. Many more modernizing European powers came to Japan demanding commerce and the leaders of the Meiji government took drastic approaches by abandoning the Confucian social and political rules of conduct and taking the European model for modernizing Japan. They especially emulated Bismarck, Germany as a role model for the fast catching-up of the modernization of Japan.

The Meiji government sent a big block of government officials for government-sponsored foreign tours to observe and learn about modernization in Western countries in a hurry. The number of officials involved was staggering, including more than ten percent of all high-government officeholders and it was an ambitious investment of a chunk of the government budget. Hundreds of the government officers took the tour and gingerly recorded their observations and learned to accumulate the knowledge and experience for modernization of the mother country undergoing historic reform. For acceleration of the reform movement, the Meiji government even hired foreign experts-- engineers for industrial plant construction and transportation infrastructure and even military instructors to speed up the modernization. Also, in a surprise move, the Meiji government started nationwide conscription in 1873 to overhaul the military system with the hope that they would become the most powerful nation commanding the Pacific and Indian Oceans.

The chain of modernizing actions were not all perfect creating protest demonstrations and even Civil War. For example, in their overambitious zeal for quick mobilization, government leaders prohibited their traditional sumo wrestling festivities, saying it looked barbaric and was a waste of people's time and energy. When anti-government demonstrations erupted for stopping the sumo wrestling, the common-people-oriented-government quickly changed its policy to combine the modern advances with traditional values for more united modernization for a long-range national plan. The government's enlightened leadership to protect the interests of common people played a pivotal role in the miraculous economic and military advancement and modernization of the backward country. Park Chung-hee noticed that the Meij thrust for modernization came mainly from government-centered leadership, yet the government tried to combine the private-sector initiatives and flexibility for the nation's industrialization. They believed that family-owned enterprises could move faster and more efficiently and were ruthlessly results-oriented in filling the vacuum created by the government bureaucrats.

A great tie between government leadership and private-sector business for economic development and the inducement of private initiatives for rapid modernization has been well displayed when people see the history of a private conglomerate like Mitsubishi Corporation. That giant private corporation started its business in 1874 ready to ride the tide of the Meiji revolution. The company started its entrepreneurship with three small ships and without many other assets except the founder's ingenuity and drive for success in the profit-motivated international business arena. The corporation has grown leaps and bounds, contributing to the objectives of the Meiji Revolution in very meaningful ways by cutting through the government red tape, developing a multinational enterprise, and acquiring industrialization techniques from their overseas contacts.

Above all, Mitsubishi was a role model for private-sector participation to quicken national modernization and to strengthen military power in time for colonizing Pacific- and Indian-Ocean-based smaller countries in tandem with colonizing Western powers. Private companies had the firsthand foreign experience and they became instrumental in introducing new social behavior such as short hairstyles, the standard solar calendar and efficient work clothes. Besides private sector business operations in the developed countries, the businesspeople had exposure to the concept of democracy and citizens' rights and freedoms through the Constitution. Japanese businesspeople with multinational operations played a major role in political reform and citizens' rights and freedoms through enactment of the Constitution.

These free-spirited businesspeople became also a part of negative influence because of their corruption through their business practice of bribing, tax evasion and profitization of socially weak or disadvantaged people, the sure sign of ills and sins of unchecked capitalism. The future president Park was preoccupied with the big picture of the Meiji Revolution that enabled poor and abject Japan to become a world power in industrialization and military might in a mere 22 years. They became the proud world power no nation in the world would ignore. Japan became an unstoppable power in the Pacific- Indian Ocean basin and soon Korea became their helpless colony without a ray of hope to be independent again and to not repeat the national error of divisive political infighting and the cardinal sin of clinging to the status quo.

Japan modernized at full speed with unity and a feeling of urgency under Emperor Meiji's well-coordinated leadership. The Hermit Kingdom, Joseon, had a brief awakening of its own untenable situation because of the small group of young enlightened social reformers such as Park Young-Ho and Syngman Rhee who recognized the approaching dark storm of colonization in the world. Park noticed without fail that all the strong nations in Europe,

Russia, and America were in hot pursuit of colonizable lands under weak national leadership.

When elite Japanese leaders and intellectuals took an honest look at their situation triggered by the visit of the U.S. Commodore Perry in three large black ships with modern weapons, steam engines, miniature train sets and other modern products, they came to three fast conclusions: Japan was backwards, modernization would take years of well-coordinated effort, and attacking foreign visitors would not render a solution as Japan was powerless over modernized Western powers. The honest acceptance of reality by the political and social leaders gave Japan prompt to-do lists, thereby opening the Meiji Restoration, a revolutionary transformation beginning in 1868 and ending in 1912.

The old law of isolation that rendered a death sentence to foreigners entering Japan and local residents leaving Japan was repelled in a hurry. Fanfare and an extravagant welcome was extended to Commodore Perry and his men to avoid a war and to learn about modern items and the technology behind them. The Meiji Empire first centralized ruling power from various warring states and then changed their feudal system to modernity by aggressively studying Western countries already organized far ahead of Japan.

With a deep sense of humility and urgency, Meiji leaders dismantled the long-held social classes, including Samurais, and organized and funded high government officials to go abroad and study modernized nations on a firsthand basis in the areas of social, military, economic, educational, and legal systems. Almost half of high government officials packed their rucksacks for the long trips of more than a year to go on a long voyage to unheard-of and strange nations in Europe, America and the Caribbean. They all had a sense of mission for the country and patiently took discomfort of primitive ships and a vagabond life without wives, servants and familiar faces around them. The long historical guiding ideology of Confucius, based on the belief that China was the center of the world and its power, had to be dismantled. In its place, modern thinking of the free market and capitalism followed.

The urgent and prevailing feeling of the leadership in the empire of Japan was that without quick modernization, Japan would become an easy target of many vying colonial powers waiting in line. From Japanese officials' expensive exploration of the modernized countries in the world and their careful analysis of a few exemplary nations, they found a model country to emulate for Japan's future approach for a speedy reconstruction. That country was Bismarck, Germany. The country showed its realization with remarkable clarity that no real diplomacy existed in the international competition and state's interests. The world powers used all their strength and influence to find probable colonial targets and conquer them. What mattered to all countries was their narrow national interest. Japanese leadership clearly understood that Japan had to modernize quickly lest she become the target of the colonial powers waiting in line for any opportunity. For modernization, Japan used her elite groups in all phases of information gathering, comprehensive planning, and forcible execution of national policies and monitoring of their results.

One of the groups that got the most attention was the Samurai class. At first, the Samurais, the upper class of the four social divisions in Japan, were disgruntled as the Meiji restoration policy dismantled many generations-old social classes in one sweeping move and the government reduced the stipends of Samurais. However, the government wanted to find roles for Samurais in the historical restoration effort and luckily the modernization created new opportunity in government and in the industry where Samurais participated in droves. The Samurai spirit of honesty, justice, courage, and loyalty was what modernization required because many people, organizations and government offices had to work in a cooperative and trusting manner for good results. The Samurai class was almost 5 to 10% of the total population and they were knowledgeable about "the way of warrior." This had a major impact on modernization for building its foundation and the course to follow based on honesty and honor among other Samurai pledges.

Park Chung-hee also recognized that Korea had elite groups. Those trained by colonial authority for Japan's leadership in the world, those with deep Confucian virtues and philosophy practice for many generations, and those with advanced technology and modernity learned overseas as students or workers. Those Korean independence fighters in China, Russia, America and other countries were an undeniably elite group. In addition, the newly-formed groups embracing free democracy, socialism or communism became social elites to pull the country to their direction believing they were the patriots to put the country on the right track no matter how different they were from each other. Nevertheless, the majority of Koreans were poor, illiterate, helpless and hopeless. The poor Korean majority also had big handicaps in becoming productive members of society for reconstructing Korea because of their colonial brainstorming and learned character defects.

After careful thought, Park came to the disappointing conclusion that Korean elite groups would not be a match for Japanese elites like Samurais. The reason was that Korean elites were far fewer in numbers and their influence as Korean elites was gravely limited. Koreans in general and especially educated elites had learned character defects, the negative mindset formed by their long colonial experiences and survival skills including bribery, dishonesty, self-defeatism, mistrust, and jealousy. Without strong, honest, and consistent national leadership, Park worried, Korean elites would be more harmful than helpful for the new nation's economic development and self-defense as the elite groups would become selfish, greedy and practice "one-big-deal" (*han tang ju ei*) after the long hungry period of colonial days and Korean War years. Park and everyone else in the leadership and intellectual group could smell the bad odor of corruption, injustice, and crony capitalism in government, military, and business fields. Korean elite groups, the product of vicious Confucian philosophy, cut-throat factionalism, and cowardly survival tactics learned during colonial times could be many. In numbers, these elite groups would be a liability rather than a positive asset by creating unfair competition and instant gratification without a long-range plan.

Park had a heavy feeling about the available Korean elites whom the nation would depend upon for its survival and progress. As Japan's colonial subject who had gone through elementary school, teachers' school, and Imperial Japanese Military academies, as well as an elementary school teaching position and a Japanese army staff position, Park had the feeling deep in his mind that the colonial mindset was elaborately designed and enforced by the colonial power, Japan. He felt that Japan wanted to bend the mind and will of the people in their colony to have them fit for their need for winning war and expanding. The colonial mindset, unless altered by education and other drastic means, would be a problem for Korea for a long time, maybe generations, handcuffing any effort for economic development and self-defense.

Japan's extraction of raw material and labor from Korea for their war effort was staggering, but mind corruption, the negative mindset caused by colonial exploitation, was far greater than mere material loss. As bad seeds with colonial losers' mindsets took positions in government, the educational system, the military, the courts and the legislation, the total national loss due to these bad seeds became incalculable. The country lost time and general trust in government for changing the poorest country to an industrialized advanced country because of corrupt people in many leadership positions. Korea's old relationship with China had been less than equal partners and that relationship wreaked havoc in Koreans' minds because they closed their doors believing that China was the center of the world. The weak Korean government thought that a good relationship with China would solve problems dealing with other countries. The unequal relationship with China, undesirable as it was, did not spur motivation for change and reconstruction of the nation. The corrupt leaders and general citizenry did not care too much about national security and independence. The old gentlemanly Confucian-theory-trained leaders proceeded "as usual" with divisions, faction building, and corruption.

Besides, traditional over dependence upon the rigid Confucian philosophy for five centuries of the Yi-Dynasty created a passive and negative mindset and there was no allowance for alternative thinking for modernization and self-defense. Alternative thinking affecting the King and factions in power was construed as a death sentence. Political leaders and high government officials did not want to wake up but clung to their small turf of family and faction, like cancer cells so wrapped in their expansion at the cost of the host body, eventually killing both the host and the cancer. The worship of China and bigger countries at the cost of neglecting self-defense capability and economic development had not changed even after the colonial occupation and the Korean War failed to provide sufficient food, clothing, and shelter to its citizens.

The corrupt and unqualified political leaders in government after the new republic was inaugurated in 1948 under the leadership of the able and patriotic independence fighter Syngman Rhee failed in its honest assessment of the state of the divided Korea.

Park clearly understood colonialism was an unequal relationship between the dominant colonial powers and the subordinate colony for the economic and military benefits of the colonized powers. He felt the unfair and lopsided relationship would not last forever as the relationship would spur independence movements and, eventually, the world's recognition that colonialism would create more wars and conflicts destroying peace and prosperity in the world. Park was convinced that Korea would not be a colonizing power to subjugate other lands, and the best thing for Koreans would be the learning of lessons from their colonial experience and admitting that the best policy for the nation would be to build a strong and moral nation for its citizens that would contribute to economic and social improvement for the world.

The age of discovery of new land with weak self-defense for colonizing purposes was over and the sooner the colonies became independent, the better for the people involved, whether they were in the colony or in the colonizing metros. Park saw colonialism was the cause of World War Two and the colonial system would disappear from the world as the result of the Great War itself which required a realigning of world orders to prevent another great war. Park engulfed himself in the reading of the Meiji Restoration in Japan as the nation was similar to Korea with a feudal system and social classes but had quickly departed from the political condition of warring states and had begun modernization. Japan started building iron smelters, spinning mills, shipyards, and rail lines, and other infrastructure such as well-planned industrial zones, and communication systems. Japan conscripted young men to modernize the military. Young men over twenty had to perform mandatory military service for four years and three more years in the reserve, catapulting Japan's military to world class in a short time. Park was convinced that Korea should learn from Japan for its survival and future progress through industrialization.

At first, the study of colonial history was haphazard and skimpy, but soon Park's reading was animated and automatically extended to the full Meiji restoration period, the most important period of Japan's modernization and subsequent history. The Meiji Restoration impressed Park immensely. It was as if a ton of bricks had fallen on him. The history answered his nagging questions of "why" and "how" regarding Japan and Korea. He knew now where he was as a colonial subject, and why the Yi Dynasty representing the Korean Peninsula disappeared from the world map. He also understood how Japan could become a dominant force in the Asia and Pacific basin against modernized Western powers.

For Park, studying the Meiji restoration was more than completing a reading assignment; it became a persistent reminder of why and how Japan and Korea became what they were. It was simply pathetic to make a comparison between Korea and Japan. Korea was like an international orphan without a home base, without a nation, with the lamentable PKG (Provisional Korean Government) in a cheap rented building space in Shanghai, China, constantly worrying about secret pursuits of Japanese agents and spies to destroy the feeble bud of the Korean Independence Movement. The indelible impression and lessons of the Meiji restoration became a part of Park's brain and heart. Nevertheless, he never knew when he would come back to read it again. The important historical event became bread and butter for Park when he came to face the historical task of reconstructing the poorest country in the world as the principal of the bloodless military revolution. The small faction of Korean military under Park's leadership overthrew the inept 2nd Republic of Korea. Now, Park had to use a brilliant military uprising the country had not seen in power for eight hundred years for the national reconstruction and industrialization.

Hindsight gives us the path of the May 16 military revolution and Park's role as "the way of warrior" as the Japanese Samurais contributed to Japan's reconstruction. Samurais had eight pledged virtues and Park had them under his skin through his training at Imperial Japan Military Academies so he could apply them to his own conduct in life and now to the lofty task of reconstructing the second poorest country in the world. Samurai virtues echoed in his ears and in his heart, in his sleep and on the job: justice, courage, mercy, politeness, honesty, honor, loyalty, and self-control along with a pertinent definition of Samurai, "one who serves" to death.

Later as the president of South Korea for reconstruction and industrialization, Park read and reviewed other revolutionary events and their leaders to make a jump start for the industrialization of the poor country when the bloodless military revolution gave a new hope for the first time in many generations. While Park was launching ambitious projects such as Gyeongbu Expressway, POSCO, a government-sponsored steel company, a shipbuilding yard, and chemical plants, he closely watched Lee Kuan Yew of Singapore and Ferdinand Marcos of Philippines with the clear purpose of learning something helpful for Korea's reconstruction and industrialization effort. The Expressway project was the largest civil engineering and construction work in the five-thousand-year history of Korea with insufficient funds from foreign loans and compensation from Japan for the colonial occupation.

The Expressway project was vehemently opposed by the minority political party leaders without any vision but with cunning propaganda instincts. They alleged that the Expressway would be for the rich to go to their mansions and resorts. At the time there were no real rich people nor any resorts or mansions to tap for pleasure. The opposition political leaders used all dirty and scandal-mongering tactics to attract poor people's sympathy without any real economic development plan. This political scum mobilized demonstrators and made opposition for the sake of opposition and not for the general welfare and security of the country. These thugs physically stopped the project by lying down in front of the bulldozers and in positions for good TV coverage.

Lee Kuan Yew was a true leader for Singapore who bumped Singapore from a third-level country to a first-level democratic and affluent country with a mountain of problems including racial conflicts, communist threat and no natural resources, and limited population and land (population 1.5 million – 3 million). His leadership triggered an economic miracle and he towered over other leaders with successful national security, an economic miracle, and a successful anti-corruption campaign.

Ferdinand Marcos of the Philippines had his own brilliance staying in power for a long time, twenty-one years, with many good reforms and policies to have poor people and rich people work as one for national progress and for building many schools to conquer widespread illiteracy. However, as the smartest president of the Philippines, he was corrupt with grafts, embezzlement, and crony capitalism by involving his family and in-laws in government-created lucrative businesses and offices. Even worse still, he took his ill-gotten money out of the country with the title of the worst corrupt dictator after Suharto of Indonesia.

From those two leaders in SEATO member countries, Park

learned a few lessons. He learned that long-term political stability was a must for 20-30 years for any meaningful economic growth in the country, and corruption was the number one problem to combat. For stable growth of a country, autocratic rule or martial law might be necessary. Park kept a close watch over these two leaders while attending a SEATO meeting chaired by Marcos of the Philippines. The U.S. President Lyndon Johnson participated in the conference for the support of the U.S. campaign in Vietnam.

Park really paid close attention to the Meiji Restoration with the motto "Enrich country, strengthen army" and to two Asian leaders who were changing their respective countries. Korea was at a crossroads and Park knew he had to be a technocrat president for economic breakthrough with singleness of purpose and powerful execution of policies. Park thought his leadership had to be on a stable and long-term basis even with the prospect of fierce opposition from good-for-nothing political factions.

6

DECAPITATED BY COMMUNISTS

"We have to make a self-supporting nation."

Love and hate was the awkward relationship Park had with communism. During the chaotic and anarchic period of Korea immediately after liberation in 1945, many young, idealistic and educated people had high hopes for communism because of its strong propaganda for a classless and equal society, a mental opium for a perfect world and a Utopia for the long oppressed and poor people of Korea.

Korea had just gained freedom after thirty-six long years of Japanese colonial oppression. Park Chung-hee had an older brother, Park Sang Hee, a close brother and a mentor who happened to be an admirer of communism. He demonstrated along with his band of select, intelligent friends looking for a perfect solution for the divided and anarchic country with deep political and social problems, abject poverty and chaos. In 1946, Park's brother was one of the leaders of the October struggle, a communist-inspired violent demonstration. Unsuspected disaster hit Park and his close family when his brother was killed by a loosely-organized constabulary during a demonstration. Park's dead brother, Sang-hee had a daughter. After his death, his close friends and die-hard communists, Hwang Tae-sung and Yi Chae-bok, gave the bereaved family financial and emotional assistance. The ardent communist and dead brother's friend knew Park Chung-hee and used to give him brotherly advice while they had grown up in the same small rural village. Through the influence he had from his brother and Hwang, Park Chung-hee was interested in the ideology of communism and did not openly oppose it. The mild attitude towards communism later created a life and death situation for Park while serving in the army as a mid-level officer, a major.

In the midst of the Korean army rebellion, a brigade assigned to crush a communist uprising in Cheju Island, secret but dangerous communist cells in the army, were exposed and Park was implicated as the ringleader without real proof. Park got a death sentence for his alleged role but, miraculously, he was pardoned at the last moment by President Syngman Rhee. Again, later when Park and his team successfully led the military revolution, Park's allegiance to democracy was questioned when his dead older brother's friend Hwang Tae-sung was dispatched by communist North Korea to contact Park. Their contact was never proven and Hwang was executed as a spy to end the serious connection with communism with his family ties.

Park Chung-hee loved and respected his brother Sang-hee and his friends for being nationalists and independence fighters during the last stage of Japan's occupation of Korea. With young and progressive minds, they aligned themselves with communism because communism provided them with a tantalizing and ideal concept of a better world that is classless, stateless, and moneyless. All three had been problems for Koreans. Besides, everyone is equal in communism and what a relief it gave people tangled in *yangban* (noble class) and *sangnom* (lower class) for the long duration of the Korean monarchy. The 1848 Communist Manifesto was good enough for the young idealistic men for vision and the courage they needed to have the motherland to be independent and strong again. Marx and Engels were saints in their eyes to correct the political and social inequities of long human history. Furthermore, the ideology of common ownership was dynamite for those who had suffered servitude since the Industrial Revolution. To many common people not belonging to the noble class, Korea was hell.

Soon, capitalism hurriedly misapplied after the liberation was the cause for blame for the misery of common people and the working class. As respected brother and mentor, Sang-hee, his second oldest brother, influenced this quiet younger brother with a boiling sense of justice and pride deep inside of him. He was destined to be a future revolutionary on no small scale. Park Chung-hee's characteristic clinging to details made him search and read all relevant material he could get his hands on, ideologies he might live under, from the library of the teachers' school. They all looked for plausible answers for the motherland to bank on when the shackles of colonialism were removed. These ideologies of governing nations included monarchism, colonialism, and communism for the Korean young generation to urgently study. Communism was at the top of their list to study and emulate for the new independent nation to be born, a nation with a long history of social, economic and self-defense problems.

Democracy was not a serious topic yet because a young and impatient Korean generation under colonial rule thought that democracy could not find successful application in smaller countries. The idea of free and market-based governing appeared naive and uncontrollable for a small nation like Korea where the majority of people was illiterate. Democracy was not real and practical enough for the people and their colonized nation to find a quick solution for the aimless people without enlightened and courageous leaders nearby. Park was determined to use the time at the teachers' college to study and obtain convincing answers to questions about the beloved but lost homeland. The reading was not rapid as Park had to spend his time and energy for the main scholastic work required for students to be teachers as set by the imperial Japanese government under their curriculum vitae.

For security, Park started books on the Meiji Revolution first, a legitimate study of Japanese history and a part of the reading requirement. As soon as he started the reading, the feeling of an obligation quickly turned to an ardent desire to dig in. The reading became his favorite topic because he saw a mirror image of Korea from Japan before the Meiji Revolution. The excitement was to learn that Japan had been a divided and chaotic country, impoverished and broken, under a caste system with samurai at the top just a couple of decades before Japan's annexation of Korea. How could Japan change and redirect itself to be a powerful, united and proud country in such a short time? How could a handful of elites with new vision and courageous patriotism form a new torch behind the Emperor Meiji to lead the country in a new direction and for the new priority, spurred by the American Admiral Perry's visit demanding the opening of the country? The reading was not boring anymore because the subject was another historical event, but it was a living, palpitating human adventure Park could not but immediately be absorbed in. An "ah-ha" moment came to Park that someday he could exert an effort to change the course of his beloved country

Korea with other patriots with vision and courage.

In Japan, during the Meiji period, only a handful of leaders with enlightenment and conviction made such sweeping changes in national priorities and in common people's roles for their patriotic participation in Japan's first major industrial and social revolution. Park, young as he was, was a true realist and hated to make assumptions. For survival, Park became a cold realist and checked his emotions, his mouth tightly shut and face sternly fixated. Nevertheless, he had moments of luxury to dwell on the "what-ifs." What if Korean monarchs had been real leaders to have the revolutionary people around them to change the long course of Confucian culture and open minds to see beyond China as the center of world power? What if Joseon (Land of Morning Calm) had opened the country at the same time or just a few years after Meiji of Japan had plunged into restoration and revolution (it took them a mere twenty-three years to attain power) ?

The power was enough to annex Korea that had a longer culture and nationhood. "What-ifs" were a waste of time and endless assumptions that history never allowed, Park concluded deep in his heart. Yet, he felt another layer of frustration and rage he had to hide inside of himself for his own safety. The unacceptable life as a Japanese subject in a colonized land had to continue. He thought he had to learn more about Korea and Japan with their own culture and different paths in history. Park internalized what he read and learned for fear of direct conflict with what he pursued at the teachers' college and also, later, in the Japanese military academies. These intensive and essential Japanese institutions were for its global expansion. They commanded a top position in the world for their curriculum and teaching staff for selected smart young people to learn and advance.

Five years at the teacher's college was an excellent amount of time for him to study many modern subjects for teachers and he was fond of such subjects as mathematics, geology, history and especially the Meiji Restoration and its courageous young leaders. Park thought the time he spent studying subjects for future teachers for Japan was extremely valuable to understand how Japan became a powerful advanced nation while Korea became a backward country and eventually a colony of Japan. The understanding gave Park a new sense of direction for his adult life, first, as a teacher at Mungung

Elementary School with a new zeal and a romantic idea that he was teaching poor but smart Korean young children for a bright future for them and also for the country to be free someday. He thought he was training future Korean fighters and not weaklings. Park was so enthusiastic with his work and his love of students, he made it a rule to blow his meager trumpet he bought in Taegu while attending teachers' school to wake up students and bewildered village people. His shyness temporarily disappeared and in its place, his eagerness and leadership showed its brilliance. Soon, he realized the teaching under the Japanese colonial agenda put strong limits on what he could teach, and how much it could influence the Korean students. He hated the obvious limitations Japanese authority put on him and abhorred the helpless feeling of being a colonized Japanese subject.

In dreaming for something bigger in his future, Park felt that his job as a teacher had an apparent limit and the subtle contemptuous remarks from Japanese superiors and even local policemen did not go away. He felt that hushed words of *josenjing* (racist Japanese word for Koreans) were clearly audible. Park thought it would be necessary for him to join the Japanese Imperial Military Academy for recognition and power. He wanted to be in such a position that people, Korean or Japanese, would not dare to look down on him. He wanted to be a part of a power that restored Japan to the present glory and the higher hegemony in the greater Asian and Indian Ocean basin. His father, Park Sung-Bin, and mother, Bak Nam-Eui, however, arranged for and insisted at the age of eighteen that he take a bride, 16-year-old Kim Ho-Nam.

His status as a married man did not steer him away from his big dream to be a part of power even though the colonizing and good-for-nothing Japanese people still called him *josenjing*, a degrading name like SOB (son-of-bitch) that deeply cut through his heart. He was in a rage but controlled it and hid it deep inside and was determined to align himself with power rather than just accepting the demeaning and abject status of a colonized people. Soon he found an outlet to join the Military Academy of Manchuria with a letter of recommendation from the military drill instructor of the teacher's school who had recognized Park's ambition and sharp mind along with his quiet discipline. The drill instructor, a colonel, thought for Japan, Park would be a good candidate for the Military Academy in Manchuria and its admission requirement was somewhat less than the

Imperial Military Academy in Tokyo,

The main Imperial Japanese Military Academy was a dream and magnet for brilliant Japanese youngsters. The Military Academy in Manchuria was a secondary yet highly institutionalized military hub and represented the will and commitment for the Japanese aspiration to dominate China's mainland and the Asian Continent. The Academy had all the national support and resources to make the institution an enviable military outpost. For the geographical reason of easy access by train and easier admission requirements, many ambitious and brilliant Korean youngsters tried and were admitted to the organization to become well-trained military leaders with rank. Their future appeared bright if Japan were to be continuously successful in its military power and domination of the Pacific and Indian Ocean and abutting land mass. These Korean military aces had to change their names, accepting the Japanese integration policy and their Korean characters were diluted day-by-day to become the core Japanese military leadership.

At the mature age of twenty-three with three years' teaching experience Park enrolled in the Manchukuo Military Academy and concentrated on harsh and regimented military training that included studies of the military system and technology. The modern curriculum offered a vast collection of knowledge: physics, mathematics, chemistry, biology, and other technical courses in addition to humanistic subjects like law, history, and even religion to be a well-rounded officer in the burgeoning Japanese military echelon. The college-level education also added invaluable training on martial arts, horsemanship, weaponry, and platoon leadership. Park's devotion and concentration to the academy training with singleness of purpose produced an amazing result.

He graduated as the first in his class and had the honor of receiving the coveted gold watch handed down directly from the Manchukuo Emperor, *Puyi*, a Japanese puppet to fulfill Japan's colonization strategies. As a part of his rewards, Park also had the privilege of continuing military training at a highly improbable place for Korean descendants, the Imperial Japanese Military Academy in Tokyo.

Park's graduation from the military academies gave him two immediate tangible career rewards after the long uncluttered hard work to get away from the position of a Korean weakling in a colonized land. The first was his commission as an officer of the Japanese Army, an undeniable symbol of power, and the other his connection to the Korean alumni of the elite Japanese military academies. The alumni connection became a source of support and networking for bigger ambitions, and even saved him in times of life and death conundrums of his military and revolutionary career. Park worked at a low rank as a lieutenant of Manchukuo assigned to a Japanese regimental commander's inner staff. He was somewhat insulated from the operations of field engagement and was fearful of direct conflict with Korean independence fighters in the vast theater of the Japanese Imperial Army in Manchuria. Luckily, killing of Korean by Korean was not in store at the moment.

Park's military assignment in Manchuria was short-lived. The last stage of World War II was fast approaching as the Allied Forces were victorious in Europe. The Pacific Theater was gaining momentum as General MacArthur's forces put more battle-hardened troops and more devastating weapons in the theater including the top-secret atomic bombs. The combined troops of air, land and sea were fast approaching the Japanese Mainland. And sooner than everyone's expectations, the war with Japan was suddenly over when two atomic bombs, one in Hiroshima and the other at Nagasaki, proved that it was in vain for Japan to continue the war with America. Park was at the mercy of providence when he was miraculously rescued from the train bound to the victorious Russians near the border. Russians who sent many German prisoners to Russia were also ready to send captured Japanese officers to Siberia and a certain gulag. Park was saved at the last minute and returned to his beloved motherland and to his farming town in rags and in a complete emotional breakdown. Park had to wait for a chance to reload a new fighting spirit in hiding and in the care of his poor family who had gotten poorer and had worsened since he left for Manchuria.

Nature abhors a vacuum. In the same vein, the political reality in liberated Korea allowed no vacuum. The country was undergoing profound transformation from the irresistible forces of the two occupying superpowers and from mushrooming local political and economic factions. Factions appeared overnight as independence fighters were returning from their long overdue foreign exile. Because of the long colonial restrictions, no individual or institutional preparation was found to deal with the independence and as soon as the colonial power was gone, an enormous chaos and political empty space were created. Along the 38th parallel, two superpowers with diametrically opposed agendas and ideologies for their occupation of the divided land were hard at work to solidify their positions while local Koreans and returning independence fighters from overseas found themselves divided into three political groups: communists, democrats and nationalists. Because of the two occupying forces, the U.S.S.R. and the U.S., the division of the country into North (communists) and South (democrats), was already a foregone conclusion for the Korean peninsula.

Nevertheless, the handful of nationalists tried to devise a unified approach for one united nation adding more confusion and animosity with beliefs that each faction was more patriotic than the others. Demonstration after demonstration was held for different purposes and became violent. As a consequence, the situation created more chaos and bitterness for the people who had suffered thirty-six long years of colonial oppression and servitude. Already, young and educated Koreans had pockets of resistance in Korea and used the communist agenda for their organizing skills and propaganda efforts. They were underground during the last few years and during the chaotic period of liberation to escape capture by authority. The Provisional Korean Government (PKG) exiled in Shanghai, China served as moral support for the movements. Park accepted his brother Sang-hee's role in the independence movement with his close friend Hwang Tae-sung as noble and patriotic devotion but with communist leanings.

Upon independence of the country, his brother was involved in a communist inspired demonstration against the occupying U.S. Army Military Government in Korea (USAMGIK) during the October struggle in 1946 on the matter of trustee governorship of Korea supporting communist North Korea's stance. Disaster hit and Park's brother, a mentor and father figure, was killed by South Korean police constabulary during a fierce demonstration. He left behind one daughter. Park's friend Hwang, the co-leader of the demonstration, evaded police capture and went over to North Korea.

From 1945 independence to 1948, the beginning of the Republic of Korea, the country was in chaos but in that chaos, Park found his renewed career of military service through his contact with alumni of the Japanese military academies. Park enrolled in South Korean

Military Academy as a second-class in 1946 and graduated with honors. He served in the Korean army with the rank of major when an army rebellion took place during the Cheju Island Rebellion mop-up operation. General Paik Sun-Yup was the commander responsible to put down the grave army revolt involving a few thousand soldiers within months of the inauguration of the new Republic with its first president Syngman Rhee. The rebellion was the most serious armed uprising to question if the infant nation might survive. The government had just seen Syngman Rhee inaugurated with his hand on the Bible as the first president of the Republic of Korea. The miracle nobody expected to happen happened. The miracle to establish a democratic republic was not in people's minds because of the brainwashing influence of five hundred years of monarchic rule and thirty-six years of colonial living.

Park was an army major assigned as General Paik's staff officer and they had long mutual respect going back to the Manchukuo Military Academy where Paik was Park's senior. But, soon, Park was implicated as the military chief of the Communist underground organization in the South Korean army. As part of the cleaning operation of the South Korean Army, Park was arrested and found guilty of being the head of military matters of the underground southern labor party in the army with an assignment to infiltrate the Military Academy with a mole implanted for future operations. Park was given a death sentence for his involvement.

At the time, the new country was struggling to establish a democratic and free-market-based republic where power comes from the people. In 1948, the southern half of the country was struggling to start a new nation with lofty goals of democracy and freedom. Park was caught at the worst time of the new republic and the punishment was harsh for anyone going against the government. The death sentence he got was not unusual as many officers tinted with communism were executed and disappeared like the dew in the bright morning light. Park was a bit different as he was not active in the communist underground organization. He was approached by the communist organizers knowing Park's brother and his background of communist involvement. In fact, it appeared Park joined the South Labor party because of his desire to avenge his brother's death by police. He also had deep seated curiosity about what communism might do for the divided country whose life was like a small flame flickering before a gale windstorm. His dead brother was a father figure and he was a local leader of the Labor Party with his friend Hwang. Hwang and another local leader, Yi Chae-Bok, took the bereaved wife and her daughter into their physical and emotional care. And Park was moved by their friendship and camaraderie.

In this emotionally weak state of Park's mind, Yi Chae-Bok, a new generation of diehard communist in his zeal to recruit more party members, presented a secret application form. Park could not refuse the application out of his appreciation of their goodwill of helping his sister-in-law with a young daughter. Besides, he had deep disappointment of the current political wrangling in South Korea by many factions. Park felt he was avenging his brother's death by accepting the South Labor party membership. Park's military background was apparently considered a bonanza by the Southern Labor party leadership which desired to infiltrate the South Korean army organization. Park halfheartedly responded to the Labor Party membership in 1945 and he did not expect that his response would become a life-and-death nightmare in 1948. Park was arrested for his underground connection in the army and he cooperated in the investigation of the underground communist cell organization in the South Korean army. The new government under president Syngman Rhee was hurriedly organizing the army with the help of U.S. advisors. Park turned over the underground organization chart to the investigating authorities for complete cleaning of communists in the army. Park's life-and-death matter was favorably resolved when President Rhee commuted Park's death sentence at General Paik's recommendation. Park left the army.

It is a privilege to see things in hindsight. It allows us to see historical facts or personal momentum with a clear view and concrete path of events. The crucial peaks and valleys are clearly noticeable when the chapter of history or the life of a great man comes to a sudden close. The period of Park's life with a death sentence for his involvement in the communist underground organization was too strenuous for him to see his own future. The commutation of his death sentence and his departure from the military were clearly a deep valley, too steep to walk up to his safety. At this juncture in his life, what happened appeared to carry less weight than what did not happen in the scheme of things. What happened to Park gave him a new lease on life when other young army officers evaporated in front of the hurriedly- organized firing squad.

What did not happen to Park, though, had more lasting impact on his life and his destiny as a revolutionary who would become the kingpin to alter the course of the same old poor country for the first time in its 5,000 year history. The cause of what did happen was not because of one factor or a personal decision. Multiple factors and conditions were at work for what did NOT happen as another epoch-making incident occurred a dozen years later. Here, what did not happen was almost providential. Park did not say goodbye to the military for good out of his complete disillusionment and frustration after his termination from the army. The death sentence on him was commuted within a hair's width of execution and that alone was ample reason and excuse for Park to forgo a military career.

He could have tried to make a living as a private civilian once and for all, thanking God for the chance to survive from the major army cleaning operation. Park did not leave the military and within a short time of changing his clothes, he volunteered to work as civilian help in the army intelligence unit without pay. Respect and trust from Park's army buddies and from those Japanese Military Academy alumni in important positions in the army gave him more time to get back to military service at a crucial time of the country's existence. The fast-moving country for a full-fledged government operation mysteriously gave Park a desk in an army where he could breathe like a fish. In the water once again, figuratively, the fish survived and looked for a better time.

The better time came in no time at all when North Korea under Kim Il-Sung's dictatorship invaded South Korea with columns of Soviet-made tanks and battle-hardened Korean troops released by Red China after the war in China's mainland was over with the communist victory. Because of their speed and battle readiness, the crack North Korean troops had a nickname of "flying paratroopers." The ferocious Korean War came in less than two years of Syngman Rhee's democratic government and the country was ready to crumble at any moment from the massive invasion from the North. The U.S. President Truman's quick decision to defend South Korea and the UN Council resolution to send troops for Korean defense from twenty member countries gave a hope for South Korea to survive.

Now, the country needed every able body to build armed forces to stop continuous communist southward movement. The experienced and motivated Park was called to lead the battle with a new commission of active duty officer. Park fought the war in many capacities as an intelligence officer, and as an artillery and division commander. Park had a fast promotion to the rank of Major General surviving the brutal war that sent too many soldiers to their untimely deaths. Park had the baptism of brutal and fratricidal war with deeper understanding of what communism meant for the country and he himself and was ready to attack bigger things for the country he loved with an unfathomable love.

For a dubious purpose, the Southern Labor party, the communist subversive and political arm in South Korea, tapped Park Chung-hee as its secret member with a glaring high title in the communist party as the chief military commissar. The secret communist underground organization wanted Park for his military credentials to recruit other members in a propaganda gimmick. The organization gave Park the impressive title to cut off Park's escape from them. Park soon noticed that the communist operation was based on secret policing and controlling individual members. The party had their members watch and check for any words or actions against the communist ideology. If anyone was suspicious, the party higher-ups did not mind using threats, coercion, even death sentences in absentia. The party functionaries always clandestinely plotted, schemed and lied to achieve their objectives and in doing so exploited whomever there was in the party with positions in the newly inaugurated democratic South Korean government.

The communist party placed its moles in the South Korean army with all reasons, flimsy or not. The party inspired the moles with hatred, aggression, and belligerence toward people in the south of the 38th parallel as traitors opposing unification of the Korean Peninsula. The communist party operatives were dedicated and well-connected with secret cells in every important organization: military, police, the Assembly, courts and school systems. They wanted to take advantage of a large segment of people complaining about extreme poverty, no jobs, no security, and an utterly fractured society in the infant government. The new government had not much resources, yet it embraced hope of freedom and economic progress for the people living in hand-to-mouth poverty and despair.

Using intense propaganda and false indoctrination of college students and army officers with their promise of communist Utopia, the communist fifth column in the south attracted a good many intelligentsia and educated people including college students, soldiers, and government workers with the idea of paradise: a classless, moneyless, and even stateless society living in equality with state-guaranteed jobs and a decent livelihood. This was a pleasant song from Heaven to those naive and innocent people in South Korea without understanding about the workings and ruthless communist domination on the Korean peninsula and elsewhere in the world. The hardcore communists and their propagandists imprisoned the minds and souls of young people and soldiers and constantly incited them to start rebellion and overthrow the infant nation struggling and organizing for its survival under the lofty goal of democracy and market economy. Communists in hiding were really able and singleminded to contact more people with complaints to turn them to their side.

The underground communists openly provoked the people, soldiers and government officeholders to break the law and order to create civil disturbances for the purpose of destroying people's trust in government and its police forces. Communists instigated more violent demonstrations in the big cities like Seoul, Gwangju, and Busan, always emphasizing the communists' roll call saying, "The end justifies the means." For the communists, nothing was off limits to take over the nation in close coordination with the completely centralized communist regime under one ruthless dictator and the Soviet puppet, Kim Il Sung. Kim was the propagandist and the notorious plotter who was well- groomed by Stalin and his henchmen for the sole purpose of Soviet communist dominion of the world. Kim had a great plan for an all-out invasion of South Korea with the help of Soviet's war materials and Red China's battle-hardened Korean contingents numbering a few hundred-thousand.

Park recognized that communism was great in theory but it did not understand human nature resisting strict conformity and tyranny, without which communism would not succeed. Park saw men exploited other men, and the weak exploited the strong in the name of communism and paradise for laborers, farmers, and soldiers. Communism was death of the soul and in its place, a material view of the world controlled people's minds and lives. No religion, no private property and no individual rights to pursue their happiness could find a place in communism. No life existed in communism, only struggles and class war. Park, after the pardon of his death sentence and his return to the South Korean army to fight the communists' invasion along with the U.S. and the U.N. Forces, had more time to observe the democratic system and free market economy with more interest and approval. Democracy and free market system do not create perfect government, but the system is more amenable to real people, real life, and their pursuit of peace and happiness.

Park also experienced the American culture and their government system, producing an environment of freedom and prosperity to its people. Park was at Fort Sill in the U.S. for his training after the armistice agreement was signed. He retained a deep impression as a general of the American people and the system providing the most good to the most people. The idealistic and naive hope and belief he had in communism had to be replaced sooner than what he expected as he went through the cold and unforgiving reality of the false propaganda of communism. Communism propagandized to have proven and magic methods to solve inherent human problems like class struggles, money problems and conflicts between nations. Was it true or just loud theory without any possibility to keep its promises? The theory does not understand humans as they are but communists believe humans can be changed by the theory. It is like putting the cart before the horse. It is also like treating cancer in the body. Communism does not mind killing the body to control and kill the healthy cells. What good is it if the body is killed to remove the cancer?

A perfect world does not exist but communist propaganda lies about its existence by class war and communists' ingenuity. Human nature does not change and communism does not improve humanity through the logic of "the end justifies the means". The communist higher-ups used that rationalization to push the communist agenda wherever and whenever to achieve their objective of one- class domination, that is domination of the proletariat. The communist party and its bosses used whatever tools available first to secure the communist regime's safety and security. Then, they used it to remove the enemies of communists: the landlords, small business people called capitalists, and intellectuals. In their place, people saw comrades, commissars, secretariats and tyrants, much more paramount positions and powers to kill and maim any reactionaries. No spiritual or religious humility could co-exist with communist extremes.

Freedom from landlords and capitalists was changed to slavery of the man-made behemoth called communism with vengeance, hatred, and enslavement of the human soul with materialism and a personal cult which ordinary people never expected. Once turning his head from his mistaken exploration of communism, Park paid attention to how to protect and cultivate democracy for South Korea and then to obtain peaceful democratic unification of the country. Park saw in himself the growth of democratic conviction and in the nation exerting its effort for the mass education of people and teaching the young generation by putting homeroom hours in the elementary school and the community movement. Young children and community activists learned to develop and fulfill democratic ideals, debates and votes along with what freedom and responsibility really meant. Elementary school children had fun and their faces were flush with excitement in their weekly class called *Jachihwe*, meaning self-governing meeting. They held debates on sports events, election of classroom representatives, classroom cleaning assignments and many other topics on life and pursuit of happiness in a democratic society.

In many senses, Park's knowledge of communism through hard personal experience and his execution of war duties during the Korean War set him free from any misconceptions of communism or any naive expectation from the wrong ideology. He understood democracy needed time to be rooted in people's lives and in the national culture for its blessing. Park saw people become independent and self-reliant without rigid class consciousness and the fear of exploitation. Nevertheless, the character deformation by the long subjugation to colonial rule would not go away in a year, in a decade, or even one generation, or worse still a few generations. The colonial scars in people's mental, emotional and spiritual domain would remain for a long time and delay any meaningful progress of democratic free and responsible life and collective economic prosperity.

The nagging colonial poisons of the mind, dishonesty, bribe-taking, factionalism, and *HANTANG JUYIE*, ("one big deal solves everything") created a big social problem in building self-defense and self-sufficient economic life based on equality and freedom. The deplorable habit of self-deception and self-rationalizing would persist to make people hypocrites. For instance, do one thing before someone's face and do another behind his back was a dishonest and cowardly act, yet people justified it anyway. This was a typical bad habit learned during the colonial period for their survival in a brutally unfair and inequitable environment where tomorrow had no better hope and today was only a day to make the most of courageously or cowardly. Smile face-to-face, but hold a dagger in the hand behind the colonial masters was the detestable norm rather than the exception. An even more disturbing psychological drawback was hoping and waiting for the invisible BIG DEAL, the self-defeating logic that honest hard work did not pay. People at first wanted a fair and honest deal dealing with the governing offices and people. But, their expectation was denied again and again by the authority and people they trusted. People did not trust how long the luck or fortune they had would last at any given moment as it could be taken away at any moment without their knowledge or control.

The colonial master had all the control and tools to manipulate the colonized people and why wait for the perfect condition where fair play existed. So, when fortune smiles, let's make "one big deal," legal or illegal, for the kill. The kill was hoped to be big and last longer after paying the bribe than the time to wait for another opportunity. This mindset was not only dangerous for orderly building of a democratic country based on law and order, but also it was detrimental to anti-corruption. With this mindset, people would be corrupt and the system could not function properly respecting government policies and private property rights. The unhealthy conditions created fertile ground for a crisis environment with further hatred and mistrust between the rich with ill-gotten fortune and the poor majority of people obeying law and order.

The environment would quickly escalate to bring more extreme social and political measures such as communists, tyrants or autocratic dictatorial rule. To Park, communism wreaked havoc for both the educated and uneducated by giving a false ideal of utopia, an impossible man-made opium and tranquilizer. For the educated, communism gave a quasi-religious-like faith to push the ideal without knowing whether the end results would be worthwhile to support. For the uneducated, communism led to blind cruelty to crush uncooperative and opposing individuals by labeling them as reactionary and enemies of the proletariat, the laborers, soldiers and farmers. More people were killed and maimed in the building of the Utopia, an illusion to be used as bait for certain failure. The end results of communism were unsupportable and pointless by destroying humanity for a temporary feeling of justice and equality.

Nevertheless, the communist ideology was so powerful and attractive, its followers tried to invent any and all means to bring about the end results. Ordinary people without the extreme fervor for communism were no match against the communist activists who did not mind using violent and threatening means of attack, killing and mind-twisting. The lure of communism was so strong and powerful to deny more decent and humanistic input from the majority of people. Communism was a magnet in poor countries in Europe, Asia and Africa where corruption of the ruling class or the government officials drew the people and the intellectuals, especially the young and idle ones. Korea was not an exception. North Korea occupied by the Soviets who had their henchmen hand-picked and intensely brainwashed by the Soviet Red Army immediately became fertile ground to plant communist ideology. Kim Il Sung and his cronies were ready to inaugurate a regime, one of the most dictatorial and personal cult-worshipping in the world, to enslave the helpless people trapped in the North.

North Korea was in a position to take advantage of their common border with Soviet Russia for quick import of aids material and military hardware for successful communist rule of the northern half of the Korean Peninsula. South Korea was, in a way, a mirror image of North Korea and it had limited sovereign power of its own with the U.S. control of the land until the Republic of Korea was formed. Thus, the extraordinary confrontation of the entire world was forming on none other than the Korean peninsula, one side for communism, the other side for democracy, starting the Cold War with a brutal hot war in wait.

Even with strong and heavy influence from the U.S. for military matters and on democracy with a market economy, South Korea did not enjoy a monolithic and exclusive single political ideology as in the North. South Korea became a violent field of the political and ideological struggle because communism and nationalism for a unified Korea persisted there. In South Korea, nationalism was a powerful appeal in the absence of centralized political muscle like in the north where Kim Il Sung had a power grip with the help of occupying Soviets. People and those Independence leaders returned from overseas exile, mainly in China and the U.S., were mired in the political infighting witnessing daily confusion and violent demonstrations for any or a combination of democracy, communism, and unification or nationalism. -Ism, -ism, was not what Koreans wanted after loss of their country for so long. What they wanted was a united and peaceful country.

In that complex political rope-pulling game of plotting, bullying, and overpowering each other, a democratic system of government was put forth by the long visionary independence fighter Syngman Rhee with higher education in America. He single-handedly tried to build national consensus for democratic government in the South alone with the backing from the U.S. government and the U.N. Charter on Korean Matters.

Park Chung-hee realized early in his military career that a compromise or finding the middle ground between the communist North and democratic South would be difficult, almost impossible. Park learned the hard way through his involvement in the communists' South Labor party, the communist underground cell in the democratic South. The whole purpose of the underground communist -organization was to overthrow the democratic government in the South for communist control and ruling of the entire Korean peninsula.

Many politicians, academicians and common people believed a compromise between the North and the South could be possible based on brotherhood, one race with the same culture and tradition, the same language and even same cuisines. Nevertheless, Park could not find any encouraging ingredient and elements for compromise. His safe assumption was that the two divided nations of the same race would remain as enemies, fierce enemies without any meaningful give-and-take. He saw no possibility of unification until one side collapsed and absolved to the other. It is All or Nothing coexistence until one side shows overwhelming superiority in military, economy, international diplomacy, or spy infiltration, triggering the demise of the other side.

In preparation for military revolution with his team of young officers and also after a successful award of the governing power through the bloodless revolution, Park paid attention to and analyzed revolutionary leaders in other countries. Park looked to such places as

America, India, Turkey, and European countries like Yugoslavia, Poland, Hungary, and others. He extended his analysis also to close-by Asian countries with remarkable historical similarities like Singapore, Taiwan, the Philippines and Japan. Park was surprised to see, in the initial stages of independence or economic development, these Asian countries were strongly attracted to the idea of communism as a viable political alternative exerting enormous power and influence. Park paid special attention to the independence leaders like Chiang Kai-shek of China, Lee Kuan Yew of Singapore and Ferdinand Marcos of the Philippines who were all communist sympathizers in the beginning and believed communism could help their independence and new nation-building. But as communism bared its dark side of dictatorial brutality, a material view of social relationships and violent class domination, they all quickly changed to democracy as the solution to their political independence and economic progress.

Park came to the crossroads of communism and democracy rather quickly and convincingly with good sense of his future direction with regards to his political, economic, and spiritual awakening and pursuit. Communism was not and would not be the solution for his problem-solving of the country he was born in, loved, and was committed to for its freedom and prosperity. He believed the country's rightful standing in the world would not be as a third- or fourth-rate poverty-stricken nation without enough food, shelter and social services. Not only survival of the democratic system of the country but miraculous economic progress would have to come sooner rather than later for people in long suffering. The discrepancy between rural and urban development and economic development without natural resources had to be addressed immediately in the face of another catastrophic armed invasion from the communist North under dictatorship and total cult-like control of the people. Park knew communism would destroy private property ownership and individual liberty as he saw in his military career. He also knew it was private interests and business entrepreneurship that created jobs and social fabric for good civilized living, not the government bureaucracy.

For Park, communism was a real loser and he braced himself to protect and to support democracy and the market economy for the progress of the country. He asked himself, nevertheless, if the individual and collective character flaws, the remnant of colonial minds of Koreans, would be a problem for his lofty goals for the country or not. Park was ready to take risks that might give new hope and strength to his loving country.

7

REVOLUTION

"Until when do we have to live like this?"

Corruption and ineffective government operation were clearly evident when the founding father of the new Republic of Korea, Syngman Rhee, became old, eighty-five years old, and was surrounded by a curtain of corrupt and greedy politicians. The brutal war and the ensuing decadent capitalism after the war produced corrupt politicians and a system of bribery and social and economic injustice. The country was slowly reeling from the immense destruction of life and material by the war with more than four million human casualties and a heap of rubble in Seoul, the capital city.

"Until when do we have to live like this?" was the burning question all along in Park's heart watching his farming family, his village, and people in the country living in absolute poverty and a negative world. Even though the country was agrarian-based without manufacturing and heavy industry it could not produce enough rice, poultry and meat products. With three sides of the country abutting the ocean, even fish and other marine products were in short supply because of an inefficient and costly transportation infrastructure. Except smaller segments of more affluent people, Park noticed people were on a natural diet and had barely enough food, and obesity was not a problem. In fact, fat people were rare and if found on the street, people would call them *sa jang nim*, a company president, an automatic reaction and instant recognition of their wealth. The funny title represented the sorry state of the country, the second-poorest country after India in the world with a GDP (gross domestic product) of $87 per capita.

The new country that had suffered thirty-six long years of

Japanese colonization could not see any economic and material benefits even after 1945 independence. A catastrophic situation came to the new nation-building South Korea because communist North Korea invaded the south in less than two years of government establishment with overwhelming weapons supplied by the Soviets for the brutal fratricidal war. The country turned to the Stone Age from the three-year Korean War which caused total casualties of four million people on both sides. The state of the country was really hopeless and people barely lived with food aids from the United States, the surplus agricultural products of all sorts: corn, wheat, long grain rice, milk products, animal and plant oils and other ready-to-eat food products generously donated by the sympathizing public.

People's need was not much. They wanted the simple basics of life to maintain their families and themselves. For many years, even generations, the majority of people had to live without any luxury to get fat, not even enough food, convenient shelter, and comfortable clothing. People lived without a fair and equitable social or legal system. If you had power or belonged to a noble class, you lived without being productive or getting your hands dirty. They lived generation after generation under autocratic monarchs who were supposed to protect individual rights and freedom. They lived under some sort of oppression all the time from social class division, from a hierarchy of rulers ranging from village chief all the way to the king. Even after the monarchical governments, people had continued oppression, from Japanese colonial rule and trampling, and later from the brutal ideologies and their communist henchmen and the corrupt disciples of corrupt and greedy capitalism. Patience and persistence became Korea's character traits out of necessity and as survival instincts to overcome the harsh and unrelenting historical realities.

These positive traits were more than balanced by negative character liabilities as individuals and as a nation. Patience and endurance were the armor to depend upon when there was nothing much to expect from the careless government for a long period of time. For survival, strength is essential and in real life, strength consists of patience and endurance. Their cumulative liability was staggering on individuals and on the country facing unprecedented complex problems after a 36-year-long colonization effort by Japan. Resistance had a limited value because Japan was the superpower in the eastern hemisphere with military might and an advanced social system to rule. The collective liability was so great that the nation-building efforts after independence became a moot question. In addition, diabolically different political ideologies, communism and democracy, came down with brute force, draining all the strength and power of self-reliance as soon as the brokered independence came to the Korean peninsula between the two victors of WWII, the Soviets and the U.S.

The condition was as if a reserve reservoir was constructed without a source of water. It was an utter empty cell collecting nothing but decaying waste. The collective liabilities alone could be a game-changer making or breaking the effort to build a nation. The collective liabilities that were known as the defects of Korean character were shamelessly vouchered and emphasized by the Japanese Resident Governor upon his departure from Korea after Japan's unconditional surrender to the U.S. possessing atom bombs. The Japanese Resident Governor's unabashed comment was that Japan would not worry about Korea as their competitive neighbor because Japan had planted a colonial mind in every Korean and his organizations. The Governor referred to colonial minds as negative elements like self-doubt, mistrust, defeatism, and dishonesty. With such a mind, he ventured to say, Japan had nothing to worry about regarding Korea's independence and restoration.

Adding salt to the wound, the two diabolical political ideologies put on Koreans made the future of Korea black, pitch black, because Koreans as victims of colonization had no control over two superpowers occupying the Korean peninsula. It was a foregone conclusion that Koreans had no say in building their own independent nation on the peninsula as one nation or divided along the 38th parallel set by the Soviets and the U.S. The Soviets' henchmen were already fully operating to put in a Soviet satellite state as the Soviets had pushed for in occupied Eastern Europe. One communist puppet regime on the whole peninsula or a divided country was the big question affecting millions of poor Koreans. What would be the sorry state of the country with swollen hopes after 1945 independence ?

Material loss due to colonization, and the Japanese government's systematic and ferocious taking from the land of Korea and Korean people for the Rising Sun's hegemony in the eastern hemisphere and more directly for the Japanese war effort was devastating in its own right. But the material loss was finite. The poison in the minds and in the spirits from Japanese influence, however, was far greater and far-reaching in its impact on Koreans and their future. The poisons and indoctrination pushed year-in and year-out for nearly four decades could be fatal. Restoration and correction of people's behavior and life direction was not easy, but not impossible. The virtues and good character might take years, or a few generations, to return to the normal and proud state Koreans desired. Koreans, after the independence, were cutting a big onion to see which layers were rotten.

The cunning colonial authorities tried to use all the tricks in their bag, researched and perfected by their most intelligent men in the military and academic organizations, to rule their colonized people most effectively without organized resistance and widespread underground activities. Many tricks were available to them. First on the list was to make the most of the already corrupted mind as the result of an ineffective monarchic rule heavily influenced by Confucian philosophy. Distrust, jealousy, and hatred between social classes were handy for their use for their profit. Besides, Japanese Authority put Korean informers and secret agents in Korean groups of independent movements or groups otherwise detrimental to perpetrating Japanese occupation of Korea and eventual integration of the Korean race and their land and all other things to the Japanese. Another less obvious yet conspiring tactic was Japanese officers holding colonial positions taking bribes from Koreans as they knew that oppressed people seldom report or complain about bribing for fear of repercussions.

The bribing took money or other hard-earned resources from Koreans but the habit also implanted in minds that nothing might be possible without taking shortcuts. That in turn created the subculture of dishonesty and dependence on illegal venues. Another less subtle but effective trick to control the oppressed people was the age-old technique of "the carrot or stick." Those Koreans helpful for the ambitious Japanese agenda were rewarded well and beyond expectation, creating the mentality that it was best to cooperate with Japanese authority and to belong to the pro-Japan group in all areas of social, military, and even academic fields. The unexpected big award from Japanese authority or businessmen for cooperation planted the seed of "Han tang" mentality for Koreans dreaming of a one-shot deal for a bonanza on their survival. Koreans became walking zombies nodding to the tune of the masters. The idiosyncratic behavior recurred at any place and at any time, putting the losing character defects in direct conflict with normal and healthy social and cultural growth in Korea. The social ills from the problem were contagious as people came to have the conniving self-rationalizing that other people do it, and why can I not do it for mere survival? People made the excuse that it was not a matter of patriotism or courage. Alone, how much can I do?

Three young Korean men were shot to death by local Japanese colonial officers who looked normal and peace-loving. All of sudden, they became killers in clean uniforms with long swords by their sides. The crime of the three was taking out wooden corner markers delineating boundaries of their land the Japanese were taking without compensation. Visible resistance against colonial rule deserved extreme measures as the Japanese executioners tied the violators to the wood post near the village road, then blinded them and casually shot them to death. The dead bodies were left for all villagers to see and to remember what their colonized authority would do to any visible open resistance against their ruling. For less visible things, the local Japanese officers tried to appease Korean villagers with smiles and some kind of a kind act, but at a moment's notice they became barbaric executioners for the Rising Sun. The Japanese in uniform with long swords and guns could become ruthless killers of the oppressed people who did not have protection or justice.

Disappointment, frustration and deja vu all over again were the predominant feelings and common lament people had. After the long independence fight within and out of the country, independence came so suddenly and abruptly. People were overjoyed and danced in the streets. The unbounded joy was short-lived in people's' lives as the nation's expectation for independence was far less as if expectations were fantasies too unreal to be realized. Korea's independence did not come as the results of Korean victory in the war even though the PKG (Provisional Korean Government) was ardently organized as the projection of the Declaration of Independence in 1919 and the March 1 national movement involving three million Korean organizers and demonstrators throughout the country. High casualties of tens and thousands of peaceful demonstrators occurred due to a brutal Japanese put-down of the non-violent demonstration.

Remembering the past independence movement, frustrated people, again, saw their expectations shattered. The peninsula was hopelessly divided, the northern half following communism with strong dictates from the occupying Soviet masters, and the southern half leaning towards democracy patterned after the occupying force, the U.S. The land was divided, the people were divided and even the families were divided along with the precious national goals and dreams. The resulting pain and suffering on both sides of the demarcation line, the 38th parallel, were endless with the vague hope that someday the people on both sides would live in peace and prosperity in one unified country.

Park Chung-Hee was in the thick and thin of all these hopes, disappointments, and uncontrollable happenings ever since he realized that he was one of the colonized race and a weakling. Park tried to use his time in the teachers' school and in the Japan Military Academies tormenting himself with "why" and "what."

Park's critical review showed the Korean monarchy and Japanese colonization were debilitating problems for the fall of Korea as a nation and as a race, creating progressively unacceptable conditions. The swollen expectations and hopes disappeared quickly as violent demonstrations simply added more chaos and difficulties in people's lives. The dream to live in a liberated homeland with peace and prosperity was just a dream. In reality, people's lives were getting worse with no authority in charge. All the transportation and the social services were at a complete standstill, and vociferous demonstrations backed by the flight-by-night political parties continued on the streets.

As the feasibility of a unified government by the north and the south was in complete breakdown, people had to wait for some direction in the forming of governing bodies and services such as the police, postal service, teachers, hospitals, banks and a host of other institutions. Depending on where people resided, the choice was given quickly without any regard to the affected people's wishes; in the south, a U.S. style democracy, in the north, communism dictated by the Soviets.

The new and tantalizing ideology had a charming and magnetic effect on impatient and idealistic young people looking for a perfect world, especially for a nation to be born after long suffering. The high hopes vanished quickly as the country divided and saw the building of different nations on both sides of the demarcation line set by the U.S. and the U.S.S.R. The basic tenets and ideals of the tandem nation-building was diabolical and antagonistic like water and oil without any hope of quick cooperation and a handshake. The three divided groups, communists, democrats, and nationalists, in between the two became real and grew more combatant and antagonistic against each other as time passed.

The nationalists preferring one nation on the land without clear ideology added more confusion and chaos and unpredictability. Park's uncomfortable ties with communists was an eye-opening issue for Park and the military authority with his glaring high title of the Chief Military Commissar of the underground South Labor Party. Many young idealistic officers in the South Korean Army had ties with the communist organization. Park's underground ties were beyond the comfort level and were regarded as treason especially when the Yeosu-Suncheon rebellion took to the streets with brutal killing and ferocious attack on the democratic government and its followers. Park's circumstantial ties with the communists brought the finality of a death sentence on him. The totally unacceptable situation gave Park the bloodbath of communism with its falsehood promising a Utopia but delivering shackles and death to people. " The end justifies the means," the communist's easy excuse for its lies, awoke Park and many halfhearted followers. Park had more than enough problems handling the situation by himself and he sought advice from his military alumni in important army positions in whom he had the ultimate trust.

In his final choice between life and death, he chose to cooperate fully with the South Korean Army investigation authorities by handing over the underground communist cell organization in the South Korean army that had been organized under the leadership of Syngman Rhee's government for its own defense. The ensuing critical events in Park's life appeared to suggest the intervention of providence to save his life from certain death. Key Army leaders, including his direct superior in charge of eliminating communists, had trust in Park's true ideological alliance. Park's death sentence was commuted, he was fired from the army, and the amazing thing was he volunteered to remain in the army as a civilian adviser.

The unprecedented fratricidal Korean War launched by Kim Il

Sung, the North Korean communist dictator, in less than two years of division was the national catastrophe causing death and maiming in the country on a global scale. Ironically, though, the war turned out to be a new opening for Park as his previous training, including at the Military Academy, were sought after by his old boss and friends to find a new path of survival for the infant democratic nation.

During the Korean War, with its high fatality of soldiers and officers, Park survived and was promoted to take charge of an important command. He started to rebuild his connections with promising young officers who had graduated from the Korea Military Academy, especially the 8th class which graduated in 1950, the year that the North attacked the South with merciless abandonment of brotherhood. Park's communist ties were clearly in the past and he had what was called a "change in facing," literally meaning changing his ideology from one direction to another, from his doubtful faith in communism to the democratic pursuit.

Syngman Rhee, the courageous independence fighter from American soil, had had brave and wise preparation in the chaotic and violent period since 1945 independence to launch the historical inauguration of the Republic of Korea on August 15, 1948. The New Republic was based on democracy and the market economy using America as a model. The republic was a far cry from any form of government Koreans knew or had experienced as the new constitution expelled all the remnants of monarchic, colonial and communist imprints. The new Republic was a revolution to the old shameful past.

Park's role in the new Republican army was quiet and uneventful with his happy growing family, a contented wife and three children. With his new lease on life from his death sentence, friends and young admirers from the army officers' corps expected more active and high energy activities. Park's life in the new government under Syngman Rhee's leadership had become simple to use his long military training and knowledge to protect the people and the growing nation as a high ranking military officer after the war ended with an armistice. Park knew President Rhee well as the commander in chief and also as the president who commuted his death sentence following the recommendation from General Paik Sun-yup. Park had unwavering respect for the president from knowing Rhee's past-- a well-educated independence fighter in America, the first elected president of the

PKG, his strong anti-communism policy and his handling of the war and the historic anti-communist POW (prisoner of war) release against the wishes of world leaders.

In Park's view, Syngman Rhee was a good president for the country with unquenchable patriotism, staunch anti-communism, and education of the young and old as a national priority. Rhee, in Park's mind, was doing right things to build a foundation of the new republic under very difficult economic and defense conditions. Park appreciated Syngman Rhee's long independence fighting away from home, many thousands of miles away from his family and support base at a time when only a few Asians were present in America. Not many people from the home country or the world leaders had remote hope of Korea's independence at the time but Rhee had unshakable faith in Korea's independence, setting a good example for Koreans. In 1905, Rhee came to America as King Ko-jong's personal envoy after his release from the Han-sung prison cell for his involvement in Korea's modernization.

Rhee's mission was to gain U.S. government support to thwart the Japanese invasion of Korea. The U.S. government in their pragmatic following of international interest already had a secret agreement with Japan, the dominant power in Asia and the Indian Ocean basin, not to interfere in each other's colonial interest, Japan in Korea, and the U.S. in the Philippines. The failed mission frustrated Rhee's effort in the U.S. But his continued effort to establish a credible Korean Mission in Washington D.C was quite noteworthy.

Park Chung-hee had his own way of watching and evaluating people to work with, his superiors, associates and the subordinates whom he was responsible for. He paid special attention to respected leaders in the country and in the world and studied them for lessons to apply in his daily conduct. He respected and admired the leaders with courage and long vision to change the lives around them and their countries. For long since his formative years, he had followed Syngman Rhee, the independence leader, for his background, courageous modernization activities in his youth, and his struggles in America to establish himself as the best-educated, no-nonsense independence movement organizer and leader. Park also watched closely how he became instrumental in forming a new nation through the U.N.-sponsored free election, drafting a new constitution for the new Republic, and foremost founding ROKA, the Republic of Korea Army, to defend the infant nation. Ever since Park's literal change of his political facing, the democratic system of operation had new meaning for him as this system of government and the bureaucracy directly affected his future and the future of Korea.

Park's evaluation system of people's moral and functional capabilities was wisely based on his long years of military training, in both Japan and the U.S.-influenced Republic of Korea Army and also his experience of school teaching at Munkung elementary school, along with the lessons he gained from studying world leaders. Park's overall method of judging and understanding people was good and on the mark and rarely failed but there were exceptions. Park learned much from the first president Rhee with high hopes in his resourceful credentials as an enlightened leader, his political conviction in democracy and his personal courage to lead the mostly uneducated people with a big bag of moral and character defects learned from Japanese colonial oppression. Park, as a highly trained army officer and having gone through other rigorous training and indoctrination, saw the spectacular success of Imperial Japan. Park earnestly believed that strong, honest and consistent leadership was essential for any success of achieving national goals of independence and economic self-sufficiency.

Park was thrilled when he read about the American Revolution against the world power the British Empire with a ragtag army without guns, ships and even without enough provisions of food, clothes and medical supplies. The Americans won the eight-year-long independence war. George Washington as the undisputed commander of the Continental Army used to say that an army of a thousand sheep led by a lion is far better than an army of a thousand lions led by a sheep. In Korean history, many lion leaders led the country when the people had pride and hope for a better life. But in net, too many sheep led the country because of negative philosophy and lack of a political system of power transfer and unity. On the independence of Korea in 1945, the country had a lion leader in the person of Syngman Rhee and the future was promising if people were united with honesty and courage. The fratricidal Korean War, brothers killing brothers, sons attacking fathers and students maiming teachers, changed the political reality and social environment where the corrupt capitalists and power hungry politicians saturated the nation, further corrupting people and the system.

When the Korean War was over with the armistice, the nation was on a heap of stones and destruction. The reconstruction was slow and the national economy was in shambles, yet cunning greedy, corrupt politicians did not lose any time dominating the social organizations, especially political parties. An impenetrable curtain was drawn around President Syngman Rhee, now well passed the functional age. He was seventy-five when the Korean War broke out in 1950, and in 1960 when a massive student demonstration erupted against election fraud and political corruption, Rhee was eighty-five, over the functional age, incapable of stopping the all-too-obvious corruption and neglect to economic revitalization. Syngman Rhee had to bid farewell in disgrace taking responsibility for the nation in a big mess. The principle actors of political party corruption, the Lee Ki-bung family, had an unprecedented departure from corrupted power by choosing a family suicide including two sons and a power hungry and manipulative wife Park Maria.

Rhee's second exile to Hawaii enabled the second republic to be established by minority political party leaders in division and ineffective and as slow as ever. But from the beginning, the second Republic engaged in political and factional fighting among old and inept politicians with greed, impotence, lack of leadership to steer a national reconstruction program and unfair justice for previous political and social criminals. Crimes before the student revolution were not brought to justice and more demonstrations flooded onto the streets. Even young officers revolting against high ranking generals, who were taking bribes and illegally siphoning assets and services from the army, did not get prompt attention from the Second Republic. Common citizenry were appalled to witness the corruption and nepotism in most government organizations and law-enforcing agencies as well as the military units accumulated in three terms of the Rhee government controlled by Lee Ki-bung and his henchmen. Ja-yu dang, the Liberal Party founded by Syngman Rhee, had an influx of the worst hoodlums interested in lining their pockets, accelerating and widening the system of corruption.

Simple traveling and moving cargo by old trucks was routinely delayed because of traffic cops asking for money or some sort of bribe on the major roadways with laughable excuses. The cops said their salary was so meager that the illegal favors and bribes were necessary. Foreign traveling was rare at the time because of the hand-to-mouth living conditions, yet a handful of young people desired to go overseas, especially to America, with fellowships for advanced education and to earn money for their families. Even these young people had to go through elaborate kickback schemes to get government security clearance from the local police.

The corruption was widespread and people waited for the quick and massive correction and delivery of proper justice to criminals. However, the Second Republic was so weak and inept in running the government that people were gravely disappointed. The delay in restoration of order and improvement of economic conditions was because of the political infighting in the ruling apparatus. The political factions in power now remembered that they had to go through many lean years without power. Thus the power game started with political divisions and confrontations with rotten government practices as usual requiring three cabinet reshufflings within a mere five months of the new Republic. People were hungry and tired with all the waiting and patriotic leaders in society and the military were anxious to see something happen soon. The corrupt old government officials responsible for the election-rigging and bribe-taking had to be brought to justice. The old abortion of justice had to be stopped by brusquely taking down the corrupt factional approach to problem-solving, "You scratch my back, I scratch yours." More menacing and immediate breakdown of law and order continued on the streets of Seoul and other major cities when organized street gangs once used for political demonstrations and lynching still brandished their fists and weapons of terror openly and unabashedly.

"Something must happen," Park in army fatigues with major general insignia on his cap had a deep thought when he searched for the meaning and significance of his life by bringing about important changes for the country of his birth and in the shame of colonization. He read many times about young Japanese officers trying to bring a restoration of government through organized action in the army, now known as a *coup d'etat*. Park thought a small action might not do any useful thing as he thought politicians in the government were divided and incapable.

Furthermore, people's mentality had been poisoned by the colonial life, the brutal war, and prolonged economic difficulties as the Japanese governor once predicted in his uncanny argument that the mentality of Koreans were flawed for normal running of a nation. Park thought he was prepared mentally to initiate an organized military action if the nation would fail to function as a progressive independent one. A revolution was in Park's mind and he might have taken action earlier but he wanted clear cause for action, a do-or-die team for revolution and a reasonable assurance of success. When the government under Rhee deteriorated further, military action might be a solution, Park thought. Yet, all conditions for military action were not ripe for the historical "D-Day of revolution."

The "whys" for the revolution were clearly set in Park's mind and the team he carefully assembled with the help of his trusted main allies, especially the young officers of the Military Academy's 8th class. Now, the "what" of the revolution had to come out as the team and schedule took a definite shape and form. Revolution was the only solution for the nation to correct from the mess of the deplorable condition and problems in the making for many generations, if not many hundreds of years. Even if the problem of extreme poverty and social division might not find quick solution, the inaction and the status quo were unacceptable to people and patriotic leaders.

Change was a must and revolution by nature would bring a hope to a dismayed nation. Hope is always precious in that it gives human vitality and optimism for otherwise there would be nothing. Park would spearhead the historical adventure and what would come of the military revolution became clear to Park. He could dispel his doubt and hesitation. His team, especially those officers in the planning and execution of the military operations plan, were well-informed and knew details through discussions at clandestine meetings at private homes and restaurants. In view of risking their lives to carry out the revolution, they had two specific goals of the revolution:

—conquer poverty

—build self-defense capability

In addition to the two specific "whats" of the revolution, the change of Korean mentality from defeatism, blame games, and self-doubt was part and parcel of the revolutionary undertaking.

The die was cast.

The team of loyal, able and committed officers and soldiers aligned themselves behind the small and bony frame of Major General Park Chung-hee to cross the bridge of no return.

What is revolution? A simple definition is the overthrow of a government or social order with a new system by force. The essential ingredients of a revolution include force, overthrow, and a new system. Based on this definition, the May 16th, 1961 seizure of government power by a handful of military officers and soldiers under General Park Chung-hee's leadership is a revolution without any reservations. However, political parties and people against the South Korean government have tried to label the military *coup d'état* something less than a revolution such as a riot, power struggle or even criminal disobedience against a military hierarchy. The attempt was to discredit the historical revolutionary effort by select military members. Nevertheless, the word "criminal" might find some historical backing as seen in the numerous revolutionary attempts that failed and judging by the anti-revolutionary groups after the fact. Revolution is by no means an easy, logical and matter-of-fact event. Revolution is a total commitment, a war where revolutionaries have to make a choice between death or survival, win or lose, or live in glory or die as a traitor.

As a military man and as a motivated student of history, especially military history, Park knew well what the consequence would be of ill-planned and poorly-executed revolution. Even overthrow of an existing government would create enormous backlash. Poorly planned revolution would induce almost automatic counter-crackdown of revolution from specially trained and organized military and police forces to defend the capital, the seat of the government. Once General Park had the responsibility of defending the capital by the 1st army and the 6th army districts, Park used that detailed knowledge to circumvent any opposition to his revolutionary campaign. Park and the revolution team made the plan in minute detail in strict secrecy, first in the mind of the leader, General Park, and then a few absolutely trustworthy team members with separate task assignments. Then came integration of the plan elements at the secret conference of the core members at different places to avoid any coincidental tracking by the government agents. The team rehearsed that plan many times first in their minds, then on paper, then in the fields with critical time and space monitoring and their evaluation.

The rehearsals were repeated to change or strengthen the logic and the momentum of the historical team effort. Then more analysis continued and thorough what-if analysis was painstakingly undertaken. The planner of the revolution tried to cover loose ends and potentially cataclysmic failures that might kill the revolution. Yet, in Park and the core revolutionary members' minds, the what-if scenarios were a waste of time and totally useless as they were assumptions in the human mind and no human, wise or not, could think of all what-ifs, one of which would kill the revolution. The leaders thought that the best thing to do was to prepare the revolutionary army to quickly adjust their actions so that maximum speed and momentum would be generated to crush any what-if problems.

They believed the right cause of the revolution and unwavering conviction would carry the day. In their minds, a revolution cannot be killed even though revolutionary people who took the risk may be killed when the revolution fails. Even though the revolutionary people could be rounded up for execution if their effort fails, the revolution cannot be killed because it gives hope to the people in abject poverty and injustice. The corrupt and inept politicians were the same character-flawed people from the monarchical, colonial Japanese rule and the nasty Korean War. They were business as usual by creating various rotten factions, and putting their pockets before the national interests and security. The hope, once given to people, no force on earth can nullify.

Did Park and the core revolutionary members see any other alternatives than the military revolution at that particular juncture of Korean history? To them, no other alternative existed as they had wanted to see real change in government systems and policies after the student uprising. The uprising was ignited by a rigged national election especially for the vice presidency and pervasive injustice in social, legal and economic affairs of the country. As for the election rigging, the position of president was not a question. The contender had died before the election and the presidency was no contest.

Nevertheless, people were tired of old Syngman Rhee serving beyond a third term without much change in economic policies and with the fear that he was surrounded by corrupt people using Rhee's old age. Rhee was eighty-five. Besides, the clandestine planning of a military revolution could not be delayed for long because of potential leaks and the turncoats in their ranks. The condition for the organization of the military actions was deteriorating fast as the team members' positions in the military could not be kept the same. Their positions were subject to change at any moment, endangering the coherence of the plan. The verbal commitment of the participating military unit commanders was fluctuating as time passed because of conditions beyond their control. Still worse, the leader of the revolution, Park Chung-hee, was to retire from active duty within a couple of months, in May. This news came as a total surprise to the team, and the news threw a monkey wrench into the hush-hush revolution plan.

The alternative was do nothing. If that alternative was taken, it meant simply death. The only difference would be slow or fast death. By taking the do-nothing alternative, the revolutionary plan would be sooner or later leaked, and investigation would be followed to find the plotters. If they were found guilty for overthrowing government as active military personnel, the sentence from the Military Tribunal would be harsh, a quick death before the firing squad. On the other hand, if the plot was kept intact without any disclosure, then the slow death of the status quo would be followed with abject poverty, cruel injustice, no hope for ordinary honest people and heart-wrenching regret for doing nothing when opportunity knocked. The slow death might fall not only on the military plotters but on the long suffering populous living in distress and gloom. After some soul- searching, Park and the core revolutionary members instantly agreed to take action no matter what, believing that no perfect condition would occur by waiting. Just waiting for better conditions would be suicidal.

Park and the core members found consoling historical facts that Heaven helped those people who took action with conviction and courage to risk their names, fortune and life for a good and indispensable cause. They saw radical and pervasive changes were possible when the revolution became a fact. From his study, Park whimsically remembered that the great American Revolution against the strongest world power, Great Britain, had an initial start with only fifty-six men signing the Declaration of Independence with uncanny assurance of their necks hanging on the gallows if the revolution failed. Park even remembered the Cuban Revolution by Castro was launched by eighty-two men who believed in the cause of revolution against a corrupt and menacing dictatorial regime impotent for any social and economic change. Even a small group of dedicated people with faith and plan of action could create revolution successfully in a suffering country.

Park and the core members concluded that it was better to die fighting for revolution than just waiting. Park recognized that revolution was in the hands of young people as seen in the April 19th, 1960 student uprising, and this time the revolution would be in the hands of young army officers and soldiers. A dozen years had passed since the democratic republic was inaugurated under the strong and visionary leadership of Syngman Rhee, the founding president. Yet, during this important period of the infant nation, unspeakable national disasters occurred because of political divisions, the poor economy and worse still, the Korean War that put the nation back in the Stone Age instead of building a free, prosperous, and just nation. After independence in 1945, new collective learning by the people was very limited or worse going backwards to colonial periods or even monarchical times. Through revolution, the nation had to obtain the good collective ingredients for the new republic, honesty, fairness, personal rights and responsibilities, and, most of all, the rule of law .

Like weeds after heavy rain in drought season, the corrupt politicians, dishonest business people and get-rich-quick schemers emerged rapidly with a total destruction of social, political and legal systems. These emerging untouchables created a lawless and anarchic situation in the tragic nation after the fratricidal war with greed, selfishness, bribes, and many other character flaws learned from their or their parents' colonial living. The new freedom of democracy and free-market-based economy gave these greedy corrupt people more territory and financial deals to corrupt the society.

Park felt strongly that there was a need to re-evolve social, political and economic justice for all ordinary peoples' living conditions after the tragic and bankrupt national situation. Only with strong and unwavering conviction in the necessity, importance and justice of the impending revolution, Park thought, would the revolutionary action have a chance of success. Park, once again, questioned if the core members of the revolution had the conviction that the action of a few courageous men would inspire the majority of people to welcome and support the military revolution. To solve worsening conditions in South Korea, the fast support of people was essential to initiate the national reconstruction. The newly-inaugurated first Republic of Korea had the high goal of free democracy and a market economy. But the new republic had an unimaginably difficult start because of peoples' divisions due to diabolically-conflicting ideologies and murderous war started by communists in the north under Kim Il-sung, the tyrant and Soviet puppet.

Additionally, the government bureaucrats and people did not have enough time for adjustment and learning their ways of living as responsible citizens of the Republic. Character flaws and mind poison accumulated individually and as a nation were many and hard to be re-educated. The new Republic under Dr. Syngman Rhee's leadership had been very ambitious and visionary with programs for free education and social training to reduce first illiteracy and then to inspire people to help build a free and democratic nation, at least in the southern half of the peninsula. The government tried to build public-school buildings all over the country with very limited resources. They were like promising buds of plants and they gave an enormous feeling of hope and national pride. For the first time in Korean history, people did not feel rigid class divisions.

The Korean war in the scale of a global and a World War devastated the country in less than two years of its inception as the democratic republic. The whole social and moral fabric of the new Republic was destroyed by the unimaginable horror of the war. The moral and humane character of citizens in an infant democratic republic disappeared wholesale. When people saw unjustifiable wanton killing and maiming by bullets and the evil ideology of communism, it seemed that moral and legal trespasses for quick financial gain looked pale and unimportant. As a consequence, the corruption and social and political ills deepened to put the patient, the nation, on a slow deathbed.

Military Revolution was a remedy for the sick patient because of the speed and strength the military organization could provide for the dying nation. The country was depressed and tired. People were not able to wait for changes anymore. A wide range and permeating changes were necessary as soon as possible as small doses of medicine would not work to save the dying patient.

The long Korean history with its ups and downs, glory and defeats, had its unique story of "could have been, might have been and should have been." Yet, never before was the nation and the whole populace subject to wholesale death and devastation. The condition was grave, like a flickering candle before the gale wind of international ideology. The powerful thrust for domination either by communism or democracy was all real. Nationhood conceived with a free and democratic mind was at an extinguishing point.

The military revolution did not plan to make piecemeal changes and small adjustments of the South Korean political and economic conditions. Instead, it was to overthrow a failed political and economic set-up entrenched in various factional and party politics where personal and party gains and interest came before the national security and stability. In no other fields than in politics and political factions were the accumulated character flaws more apparent and visible. It was because the old Confucius-principled, saving-face naïve people were no match for these lying, plotting and propagandizing professionals. These hoodlums and extremists got together and saturated the political arena, yielding enormous power. Irrational and illogical people had a free hand in the economic and important political offices.

As in the economic theory, the bad currency pushed out good currency, leaving the field of politics to no-nonsense criminal elements of the society. Good decent people objected to going into politics. Slowly and definitely, the majority of the society ended up being controlled by the less-qualified aggressors. The original good but naive intention of good people had to pay a hefty price by causing a corrupt society. The emerging nation lost the opportunity to add honesty and decency to political arenas and people came to be victims controlled and denied by the very politicians they tried to avoid. The best people went to other fields such as military, technical, academic and business fields. Many eventually immigrated to other developed countries.

As good and qualified people neglected their being involved in politics and government affairs, the law and order in the society further deteriorated with bribe-taking, embezzlement, stealing, contract fraud, and worst of all, election-rigging and illegal profiting from office holding. Moral and religious values were abandoned and corrupt capitalist views of instant money rewards prevailed. Liberation from the colonial rule was over, yet the cumulative individual and collective flaws were coming to the surface without willful and national effort for correction. The infant nation that started with higher goals walked into an abyss and national disgrace, losing all hope.

Park and the revolutionary force concluded revolution was the answer for the nation in a collision course with its destiny. Revolution ought to be the answer for the reconstruction of the country and a lifesaver for the young officers and soldiers ready to move to Seoul.

8

TEAM

"Are this country's politicians keeping up their struggle for power?"

"No, we should fix them right."

"Live by order and die by order" is the military maxim that makes people in the army function as a team. The strong team is essential for military operations, especially when a group of young officers and their units undertake a revolution for the nation of some 30 million people. These people were under precarious armistice conditions, a reminder that the communists in the North might start a new war again without advance warning.

Hindsight shows a privileged view of objective events and a conglomeration of multiple facts causing a historical turning point clearly. However, in the muddy reality of action, the view was not that clear at all. In fact, the mastermind of the action was subjective and lonely. The military revolution that took place in 1961 in South Korea with active participation of over 3,600 army officers and men was not that clear and obvious to the nation. The general populace did not know how the idea of the revolution came from the mind of the unlikely general with few words and an unimpressive small and dark stature.

The idea of a military revolution had lived in Park Chung-hee's conscious mind for a long time ever since he entered Japanese Imperial Military Academy and learned about forces behind the Meiji Revolution and other group actions of young patriotic officers. The idea of Park was subjective and fluid as he grew in life and military experience. The idea of military action became more of an illusion as he started to learn the histories of Korea, Japan, and the world. His analysis of the Meiji Revolution in relation to Korea under colonial rule was subjective and conflicted with others. Subjective as he was, his idea of revolution had a staying power as the idea gave him a hope no matter how vague and faint the hope was.

For a person born and living under colonial rule, an undeniable fact was that the colonized people had an automatic judgment from the Japanese, especially public officials: a weakling, a coward. Park detested being called a weakling and being looked down upon as a race. Japan, a colonizing master, could do whatever it wanted to Koreans. He came up with the idea of revolution against unjust authority and that idea gave him a sense of dignity and reason to do his best whatever he was doing. His subjective idea slowly transformed to an objective conviction as more practical elements such as the conceptual plan of revolution, the team, and what-if analysis were added to his chain of thoughts.

The cause, the team, and the possible likelihood of success were constantly roaming in his thoughts as necessary elements of a revolution as extra-curricular mind exercises. He continued those mind exercises for many years since the military training became his life. The staying power of his mind exercise on revolution was tremendous as the mindgame gave him time to relax and fantasize about a better world for him, his family and the suffering colonized Koreans. Park's daydreaming was gaining traction with further conviction as he befriended young, smart, and idealistic officers fresh out of the Korean Military Academy with similar backgrounds and dissatisfaction of the conditions and future prospects of the nation.

The subjectivity of Park's idea of revolution was understandable as it came from a single mind when such a notion was almost impossible under colonial rule with no possibility of any success. Revolution was a team effort and no sound man would even consider it. It was just a mind exercise without any tangible input from people, organizations, or friends. The singleness of the idea was easy to handle and control when it was in one man's mind to avoid leaks or unwanted attention from any intelligence-gathering organizations. The idea of revolution was just an idea without any real form or secret documents. Yet, the idea had its own life to grow and mature with careful study and reading of successful revolutions, big or small, in the world. Well-known classical revolutions in America and France occupied volumes in libraries. Besides, the Meiji Revolution in Japan was a part of military instruction for educating Japanese army officials in military academies. More modern revolutionary incidents in

Turkey, India, and China were well-documented and their storytelling was readily available without attracting any suspicion. The story of communist revolution in Russia added another layer of information and the glory of successful revolution.

The seed of revolution was planted in one man's mind and it soon took root in the deteriorating physical environment of the South Korean government. Park's role and influence in the Korean army expanded with his acceptance as a strong anti-communist leader with honesty and many talents. One more advantage he had was his connections to his Military Academy alumni no other officer had because of his involvement in all three influential military academies at the time: Manchukuo Imperial Military Academy, the Tokyo Imperial Japan Military Academy and the Republic of Korea Military Academy. His alumni of Military Academies were the cream of the crop of Korean elites with ambition, talents and discipline. Besides, they were the best-educated and trained young Koreans by the world power, Imperial Japan, with all the resources for a modern education. Having connection to the alumni and their respect and trust was like having a tank division to rely on to defend himself and his work against possible enemy attack. Under new changing circumstances, Park thought he would render a meaningful and significant role to help the nation as the cadre of talented young Japanese officers had helped the Meiji Revolution for its shining success of restoration and lifting Japan's standing in the world.

Park thought extreme measures like revolution would be required to correct the path of the nation if something went terribly wrong in the infant nation under Syngman Rhee's watch and leadership. After all the seed of revolution, subjective and isolated in the mind of a single person, might find its use with its quickened blossom by adding trustworthy revolutionary minds from his earlier association in the military and old friends. Park wished the infant nation under Syngman Rhee to grow strong and solve the age-old problems of poverty and factionalism. Park respected the leadership of Syngman Rhee, who was instrumental in ushering in democracy and education of the long-neglected people. Park did not wish failure of Rhee's first republic for the sake of the revolution whose necessity and success were questionable.

Park instinctively tried to see the big picture and wait for more integration of progressive ideas and good vision of political leaders and the liberated people. Yet, in the back of Park's mind, a big question mark remained as to the colonized minds and poison retained in the collective mind of people and the nation. Surgical operation by justifiable armed revolt might be necessary as Syngman Rhee passed his youthful and vigorous age to face mounting corruption and greedy politicians surrounding him and blocking his eyes and ears.

Park's graduation from all three military academies open to elite Korean young men was an invaluable connection for his future move and he gingerly maintained relationships. All his associates and connections made in Manchuria, Tokyo and Seoul had been a source of mutual trust and recognition. Park's association with old military connections served him well by first saving him from a death sentence for Park's communist party membership and then by providing rapid advancement in the army. Now, Park's honesty and charismatic leadership slowly and definitely drew young officers in the army around him with genuine patriotism and complaints about corruption.

In the first year of the Korean War, Park survived and made an important family tie with a young 8th class graduate of the Korea Military Academy, Kim Jong-pil. Park arranged the marriage of his favorite niece, the daughter of his mentor brother Park Sang-hee, with Kim. His brother was killed in 1946 during a communist-inspired demonstration one year after the country's liberation when the country was in chaos tangled in the diabolical ideologies of democracy and communism. Kim was an influential member of the 8th class and served as a mid-level army officer after the Korean war ended. He and his classmates found it necessary to bring up the corruption inside the army and they made an open criticism of the army brass going through business as usual. As the nation had hiccups from the power-hungry politicians and the army higher-ups in the whirlpool of corruption, Park's revolutionary idea was still hidden deep under his sharp observation and analysis of the situation. Young officers, Kim Jong-pil at the center, brought their consensus to Park for discussion of open revolt or outright military operation to overhaul the nation.

Park became a well-rounded military commander in important posts. Park's military training with advanced science, law, and organization skills made him more effective in his command than other conventionally-trained officers lacking mathematics and number science. Park was fortunate to further his experience in the pragmatic and systems-oriented U.S. army training. For instance, the briefing chart approach used in the U.S. Army for problem identification and resolution on military operational matters was also eye-opening for the Korean army for its efficiency and more objective analysis of a situation. In a way, Park Chung-hee became a technocrat himself.

He was a technocrat by military training and being an artillery officer dealing with the advanced military technology of hardware and the delivery system. Furthermore, he had a chance to go to the U.S.to Fort Sill for six months to enroll in the curriculum for generals in artillery. He familiarized himself with the military technology advancement in artillery and systems theory for optimization. Park came to command the biggest military supply command in Busan before he was tapped to command the 6th Military district near Seoul. Park's military credentials and charismatic character was a magnet to attract elite and patriotic young officers ready to jump into the revolutionary effort. Park had harbored the idea of revolution for his entire adult life and his preparation would soon meet the reality and its destiny.

After having witnessed the ineffective government operation and cut-throat factional fighting in the Second Republic, Park and his cadre of motivated officers reconvened the Military Revolutionary Committee that had been formed before the student uprising. They reactivated the committee in secret to officially organize and plan a military revolution. The long-hidden, almost personal, subjective plotting finally saw the light of day and went beyond one man's conviction. Revolution during Syngman Rhee's government was a definite possibility if the April 19 student uprising had not taken place. Park was relieved that the revolution did not happen during the time of Syngman Rhee, whom he respected with sincerity.

Revolution is not for everybody. It is a business risking the lives of participants, especially the sure death of its leaders and close assistants. The stakes are high but the reward would be extraordinary if the revolution would be successful, changing the destiny of personal lives and that of the country. The turning point of the country's history would give the entire nation a sense of hope and new determination to solve the nation's three critical problems in a united way with the revolutionary force at the front: the chronic extreme poverty, absent self-defense power, and the people's poisoned mentality. The members of the Revolutionary Committee worked in secrecy but their careful selection and trustworthiness were in great peril as informers or weaklings in the committee would destroy the revolution in the budding stage. Park and the key committee members had many sleepless nights to keep the secret until the last minute before all-out action.

A few false alarms made the team perspire with sweat. They tried to set the date of revolution as soon as possible. The whole plan was at risk if leaked ahead of the time of execution and it might destroy the revolution in a minute or two by a call from the Chief of the Staff of the Army. Painstakingly, plans were made to confuse the military authority by hatching some sort of cleaning request of corrupted officers in the army. At the same time, a secret request was made to General Chang Do-yong, the Army Chief of Staff, to give tacit approval if a revolution was launched. The first plan was to mislead the revolution as a minor corruption cleaning operation. The second plan was to put General Chang in hesitation when he received report on the pending revolution.

Hindsight showed both plans worked to earn valuable time to launch revolution without any major armed forces resisting the revolution force. 3,600 revolutionary forces were quite minor compared with over 600,000 total armed forces, but the revolution forces carried the day. Park also instinctively accepted the necessity of studying well-known revolutions in the world. He wanted to have deeper recognition of factors that either made or broke the revolution. Success in their attempt meant glory and failure represented a guillotine and death.

Park risked his life many times in and out of his military career, a last-minute rescue when he was being transported to Russia as a surrendered Japanese officer, when he was appointed by the South Labor Party as the underground Chief Military Commissar in the South Korean army, and a death sentence conferred during the Yeosu-Suncheon army revolt on account of his communist underground connection in the South Korean army. Park was not afraid of risking his life as he had seen many gallant examples during the training in Military Academies. But this time, Park realized the consequences would be far greater than before, risking his established happy family and corroborating military officers and their families. It also put the entire nation at risk, a nation on the brink of resumed war with the North who were looking for a weak crevice in the South Koreans' self-directed crisis.

In making the team, Park envisioned three groups of members consisting of the military revolutionary committee; the core, the muscle, and the face. The core was its obvious backbone forming the body where the muscles were added and the face was powdered and beautified. In these three groups of revolutionary forces, Park instinctively recognized the peril of collaborators quickly changing their sides to save their necks at the slightest sign of failure. Friends, at the moment of doubt, could become enemies and betrayers in an instant when the scale tipped to one side, as Park had experienced in real life serving in the military intelligence units. He hesitated asking the revolutionary committee for a perfect condition to launch, but he also realized that there was danger in delays and half-hearted execution of the plan.

In revolution, there is no perfect condition and the punch has to be delivered when it should, regardless of the conditions. The plan and its execution had only one chance. Park clearly realized the revolutionary undertaking was an all-or-nothing venture and there was not much in-between. Success or sink was the mandate Park and the revolutionary committee had to face. Park thought he had to apply the common sense he acquired long since his bid for a military career to avoid the status of "weakling," a name he detested. The common wisdom was, "Take action, then necessary motivation will follow." Park was sure hesitation and too much thinking would give no advantage in making decisions and taking appropriate actions. He concluded that necessary motivation would follow and picked himself up to do the right thing. Contrary to the common notion that motivation was necessary for any major action, courageous action supplied necessary motivation to continue in the right direction.

When Park and his immediate masterminds concluded that nothing short of revolution would resuscitate the dying body of the nation under corrupted politicians surrounding Syngman Rhee, the forming of the Revolutionary committee was quickened with the following lineup:

Mastermind—Park Chung-hee, Kim Jong-pil

Core—nine original members, generals, the 8th class of ROKA, selected officers

Muscle—Army Airborne unit, the Marine corps, 6th Army district artillery unit, Army reserve divisions, the publisher, fund contributors

Face—Army Chief of Staff Chang Do-yong, ROKA Military Academy

Park learned by heart that for successful military operation the objective of the mission of each participating unit and its members must be clear. Without a clear objective, the group assigned to the dangerous operation could not generate a concentrated force to penetrate the enemy force with knife-edge sharpness. The objective of the planned revolution had to be clear in his mind first and then conveyed to people participating in the risky mission, from the lowly foot soldiers all the way up to their commanding officers. The whole force of revolution should behave like one body, Park emphasized. As the force of the revolution reached the heart of Seoul, the forceful occupation of the national broadcasting station was a priority to convey the objectives of the revolution clearly and to the point to the general public repeatedly. The public support for the revolution could not be gained unless the revolution's objective was understood and agreed upon without doubts or suspicions. The pledge of revolution was announced item by item and no room was allowed for any misunderstanding.

The pledge had six clear and definite bullet items and people paid special attention to three items emphasizing anti-communism, economic development to eliminate poverty, and return of the governing power to a civilian government as soon as the revolution's objective was fulfilled. The long-contemplated revolution had a fierce headwind at first so powerful as to nip the effort in the bud but the fever of ardent desire to change the country's political and social directions provided the staying power to change the headwind into a tailwind. For instance, the revolution forces dug up trenches in the outskirts of the city towards the Korean Military Academy and the 1st army access to Seoul to block potential efforts to suppress the revolution. The trench showed the determination and dedication to the revolutionary cause. Within days, citizens of Seoul witnessed the parade of cadets of the Military Academy in full colorful uniform in support of the revolution. This generated the well-needed momentum for the revolution.

Nevertheless, Park and the core revolutionary committee members furiously hoped that the headwind of resistance would turn to a tailwind of support as revolution soldiers with guns and bayonets took their positions in an orderly and soldierly manner. The revolution forces had arm bands with three black Korean letters *Hyuk Myung Gun,* "Revolution Force," for every young and old suffering person to see. There was a certain air of welcome on the part of general people and pride on the face of the soldiers with the armband. The headwind slowly became a tailwind to bring about historical change in the nation's helpless state. The headwind had been in the making for generations because of sick monarchism, oppressive colonialism, and devastating communism controlling the country and the mind of its people without any restraints. The poisons thus acquired had become a big monkey wrench increasing the character defects of Koreans, the stumbling block to the nation's healthy growth in all socio-economic and political arenas.

Park remembered his old experience of crossing the sea of Japan on an army transport ship on his way to Tokyo, the capital of Imperial Japan, to attend the Imperial Japan Military Academy. He gained admission to the coveted Imperial institution as a reward for his first-place graduation from Manchukuo Military Academy, an extension of the main Japan Military Academy in Tokyo. His experience was to watch small seabirds following the military steamship off and on. Park wondered how the small birds could survive the vast open ocean without any landmass nearby. Park noted the birds were amphibious by being able to land on the ocean surface briefly when tired, looking for stray fish by the side of the steamship.

Park pondered, for staying power of the revolution and its successful execution, all participating individuals and units should be self-sufficient and should survive until they accomplished their objective, be it secrecy control, or logistics of food, tent, arms and other battle gear. Park expected the worst in the initial days and weeks for survival and the staying power of the revolution, when taking over various government functions would present unmanageable problems. The arrest of corrupt politicians responsible for the crimes committed of election fraud and death of demonstrators, organized street gangs used for political purposes, and even supervising and operating national broadcasting stations could be potential problems during the initial period of revolution.

The die was cast and all involved in the revolutionary struggle was waiting for the final order of "GO" from Park, the supreme commander of the revolution ready to make an epochal turning point in Korean history. In his mind, the clear measure of success of the revolution would be the bloodless operation convincing the rest of the military units of the army and people to accept the reality of the situation in the southern half of the peninsula.

Bloodless was what Park Chung-hee hoped for and stressed to the army of revolution in their conduct of revolutionary duty. Bloodless was a goal but Park admitted that the goal might not dictate the reality always. Park was neither a perfectionist nor an idealist. His cold and calculating military discipline was in command now.

Bloodless or not, the revolution was on.

The ardent desire for revolution in one man's mind is nothing but an illusion at first. Slowly, that illusion became a reality, and inevitable action. With transformation, changes come from a mere idea, not just acceptance of a given situation. The transformation is not happenstance, rather it comes from the blood, sweat and tears of hard training, in-depth experience and unquenchable hope. The action based on the revolutionary plan that the secret revolutionary committee members drafted and perfected was only a hope and expectation on paper. The action did not have any teeth until it became an immovable faith by a series of team actions with brute speed and strength to overcome any obstacles in the way of action.

The band of brothers gathered at a small room of a private house and a heated discussion followed over typical Korean drinks like Sake or *Soju* with simple side dishes that the ringleader's wife prepared for the occasion. A half-dozen men with tanned faces were in inconspicuous civilian clothes but they were mid-level army officers on active duty. The place was in Seoul at the small private house of Kim Jong-pil. They were alumni of the Korea Military Academy, class 8. The discussion was about corruption in the political party in general and in the army specifically. The discussion was more detailed and animated when the group went over the plan to overthrow the current government. The people gathered there were part of the secret military revolutionary committee with Park

Chung-hee as the head of the revolution and Kim Jong Pil as general secretary with close and direct contact with each other. Kim was married to Park's niece, the only daughter of his brother Sang-hee, his favorite brother and a mentor.

The need for revolution was a foregone conclusion and the condition of the country was dead serious and discouraging. But the work they were planning as a team was a very dangerous mission with no safe return to the original condition if something went wrong or if the plan was aborted midway. They accepted that if their mission was unsuccessful, it would bring a harsh measure of punishment, usually a death sentence, to the key perpetrators. Soon, for the purpose of launching the revolutionary plan on the country that had not seen military revolution for a few hundred years, Park Chung-hee assembled nine key members and Kim Jong Pil to review details of the plan and potential supporters with key national positions. The key revolutionary members came from Park's three military academies he attended and Kim Jong Pil's Korea Military Academy 8th class. For secrecy, the General Secretary Kim served as liaison between Park Chung-hee and generals involved in the military revolutionary committee.

Park Chung-hee's attendance to all three military academies and his graduation as the top or close to the top of the classes became an immense help for the revolutionary planning. Park was a known quantity to many people, especially in the army, and his ability to garner the top post of the graduating classes added invaluable credibility to the revolutionary team. Furthermore, his reputation for his honesty and charismatic decision-making ability attracted many young and ambitious officers in the military. Park was effective in gaining support from generals in key positions in the army and garrison commanders with troops in the proximity of Seoul, the capital, for lightning-quick occupation when the D-Day of the revolution came. Park continued his role to align additional generals while the younger officers with Kim Jong-pil at the center were to build a supporting network at all army divisions, and 1st and 2nd army staff offices to control the chain of command at the staff officers' level.

The revolutionary committee paid special attention to army divisions near Seoul for either division commanders' support and, if not, at least staff officers' committed support for the revolutionary plan. The 1st Army was the main force concentration to protect the country from the invasion of North Korea and had more tank battalions and weaponry. It was crucial to get the support from the 1st Army or a neutral position at the time of the revolution. Consequently, the Revolutionary Committee paid special attention to the region under the 1st Army operational perimeter with potential trenches and other tank-buffering measures by placing tank traps on the way to Seoul.

Park garnered important support and troop participation from generals of the Marine Corps and the Airborne Special Forces garrisoned just south of Han River The other younger revolution committee officers were very effective in aligning important divisions which might be mobilized to stop the revolutionary troop movements. Their effort to identify and isolate potential commanders who might be against the revolutionary movement was successful in time for the revolution to be launched. Through their previous association for the anti-corruption movement in the army, the junta members used and at times manipulated the anti-corruption campaign to open real communication with the movers and shakers of different army units to ascertain their support if necessary and influence their commanders not to go against the revolutionary forces. The Revolutionary planners also cleverly used the anti-corruption campaign in the army to confuse the secret of the revolutionary plan to the very last minute

After the student revolution in 1960, more corruption scandals surfaced in every branch of government, and the military was not an exception. Many high-level officers in commanding positions got involved in daily corruption charges mainly for illegal enrichment by siphoning out military supplies and the criminal use of equipment for profit by transporting local products and raw materials. Another area of corruption was high military officers being involved in election-rigging by aggressively promoting votes in favor of specific political parties and their leaders. Military officers' ties with the political leaders produced a stench in promotions, assignment of work, and in some cases marriage arrangements for promising young officers to build their network of influence in the military and major government offices. The majority of honest and hard-working military officers felt heartfelt dismay and disillusionment in the delay of the cleaning-up of corruption. Almost all honest officers lived in the poor section of the community in an economically retarded environment, worrying about their family's housing, education of their children and even daily sustenance with their small salary. The nation was too poor to pay a working wage to honest officers and soldiers.

The contrast between the corrupt and honest officers in the military was obvious and undeniable. First of all, the corrupt officers had better duty assignments close to Seoul or big cities while the honest officers were sent to the front line close to the DMZ (demilitarized zone) without amenities and close family presence. The corrupt officers lived in the affluent section of the city with brick houses and paved wide roads. They also belonged to highly charged and influential social and political groups with connections to the Liberal Party and their cronies who had the power to influence promotions, positions, duty assignment and even matchmaking. All this corruption was done through bribes from the illegally-earned money. The smell of corruption was everywhere.

These corrupt politicians and officers had the attitude, "You scratch my back, I'll scratch yours." The private association of quasi-illegal groups tended to demoralize the entire country, especially the young generation hoping for something more just and equitable for all people. As the old Korean saying goes, " one bad fish stirs the entire pond." The private elite group clung to their connections for the selfish goal of personal enrichment and behaved like "liberation autocrats." Character defects of people learned from their survival in a colonized country were many—bribery, dishonesty, division, envy, and worst of all, *Hantang chuei. Hantang chuei* was nothing but self-deception for a short-term goal. As most people under colonial rule did not have freedom or incentive to build their own honest and proud life for a long future, people were hungry for any opportunity for the short-term goal of big money, a large tract of land or whatever was useful for survival. The colonial government was in absolute control and there was no guarantee on any long-term endeavors. So, "Why do I have to be honest and lose the chance?" was the typical justification for Koreans to indulge in *Hantang,* "one big deal."

Honesty and meritocracy were disappearing rapidly. The social and the political environment were degraded after the brutal Korean War stopped with an armistice agreement. The war mentality persisted to big and lavish living without regards to building a just and equal society in the infant nation. The nation was founded miraculously based on free democracy and a market economy with ample reason to protect the system. People with the mindset of right and ethical norms thought that a revolutionary change had to come voluntarily or by force. The smell of corruption and the feeling of helplessness were epidemic.

In addition to the desperate situation, students organizations started to behave as if they could control the political situation, including efforts for unification, after the student uprising dissolving the first republic. Some students organization tried to contact the communist north on their own initiative to open up unification without really knowing how the communists would lie, provoke, and propagandize to infiltrate and divide the democratic south and conquer to establish a communist satellite of the Soviet Communists. Student were full of energy and hope. Some of them were used by communist agents and hidden supporters to dismantle the South Korean government. Students pulled demonstration after demonstration and made demands to negotiate with the communist north for unification without knowing the danger of the national security being compromised.

In this depressive mood, young officers trained in the Military Academy had seen the gross injustice and tried to demand the resignation of their superior, none other than the Combined Army Chief of Staff, and other high ranking officers with incriminating evidence of corruption. Lieutenant Colonel Kim Jong-pil was at the center of this "revolt against seniors" with other collaborating officers. The courageous young officers had a clear sense of purpose for cleaning up the Army. Their actions served as the first experiment of group action against the corrupt status quo. By then, the initial group for the planned revolution under the leadership of Park Chung-hee had been formed for some time. The revolt against seniors served two purposes. One was the consolidation of the group of officers who would become the core member of the secret military revolutionary committee, and the other was early identification of potential enemies of the planned revolution.

The revolt against seniors created a shockwave in the army with the understanding that corruption as usual was not acceptable and that the 8th class of the Military Academy was effective to bring the revolt as a group. The group was mid-level colonels and they wielded enormous power as they served as key staff in army divisions and commands for the military training and preparedness for defense against communists or the enemies of the state. Park as a major general in the army with the important duty of a conspicuous position and with a reputation for honesty promptly gave his clear and forceful support for their anti-corruption campaign. Park's action was courageous as no other generals came to support the group as repercussions against such support could be harsh from the established military brass.

Park Chung-hee, by this action, generated resounding trust and loyalty from the would-be core members of the secret Revolutionary Committee and at the same time drew positive attention from the bulk of the expanding but still corruption-prone military organizations. Another implicit side effect was people in positions and the military leadership started nodding and admiring Park's positive character as a leader. Honesty, this was not the norm in the army and a few honest leaders drew unexpected acclaim. In the extreme circumstance of a revolution with limited time and accurate information, for the mastermind and his team, positive perception of its leader's character became a crucial factor, either making or breaking the revolutionary movement. The revolutionary committee, with its nine core members and its skeleton of organization, started to fill in the pieces of the puzzle. Prompt adjustment to the revolutionary plan were made for its effective and lightning launch.

As a part of Park's effort to connect and align other generals for the broad support for the revolution, he tried to sign up support from two important military commands but failed to garner their support. One was the CIC (Counter Intelligence command) with the duty to gather critical military intelligence and national security-related information. The response from CIC was lukewarm without intent for positive participation. Another recruitment failure was the armored 9th division which had heavy weapons capability and an ability to quickly maneuver to solidify revolutionary military occupation of Seoul. The division was also capable of blocking potential anti-revolutionary forces mobilized from the bases close to the capital area.

Seoul was critical to occupy by revolutionary forces first and foremost as all three government branches and the important national broadcasting companies were located there, serving as the nerve center of the nation. The response from the 9th division was negative and the revolution committee was anxious for possible leaks of the secret junta plan. Fortunately, neither of the two commands reported the surreptitious contact from General Park for revolutionary support out of their respect for the general known for his honesty and strong ties with influential Military Academy graduates from all three notable institutions. The failure of general Park's recruitment was discouraging and in a way disastrous for the revolutionary plan. However, the crisis passed because no report was made by the two crucial military organizations.

The core members of the military revolutionary committee and other participants included: General Park Im-hang, 5th Corps commander, General Kim Dong-ha, 1st Marine division commander, Lee Chu-Il, 2nd Army Chief of staff, General Yun Tae-Il, defense institute researcher, General Kang Moon-bong, Colonel Kim Yun-keun, Marine regiment commander, Kim Jong-pil, Lieutenant Colonel, retired, and his selected classmates.

As the revolutionary plan came close to the point of no return, General Park received an encouraging commitment of support from the mass media. The editor of the Pusan Daily News was going to provide important and essential dissemination of the historical military revolutionary effort. Mass-media coverage was an utmost and important task especially during the first few days of troop movements and consolidation of momentum of the revolution by sending necessary information to citizens, soldiers and the politicians sick in the muddy field of politics and factional fighting. More good news came. A wealthy businessman with an eye for a bigger and right government put his hat in the ring by providing necessary funds for efficient revolutionary activities requiring immediate expense and funding with a large contribution of seven and half million *hwan*.

Revolution to change the old order to a new order is like a puzzle consisting of many pieces where each has its unique place in the whole puzzle to complete the image. Each has its own importance in relation to other pieces and putting the pieces in in an abstract manner will not work. The fitting of a puzzle requires detailed work and so does revolution in even more critical ways as the action of revolution deals with brute force resulting in a life-and-death situation. In an emerging free democratic country, it is not simple to control the information flow and potential leaks of important plans always exists. Even though Korea is a small country, it had sizable armed forces, about six hundred thousand troops trained and experienced in a brutal Korean War. A small segment of the armed forces might be able to control the country for a short period of time. Even that needed consent from the rest of the armed forces.

If a sizable force had been mobilized to block the revolution, a successful revolution would have been in great danger and might have created civil war. Consequently, the revolutionary plan required minute-by-minute operational detail in all aspects of planning, organization and execution. If the revolution required details, it was blessed to have General Park Chung-hee as the commander and the mastermind. Park, all his life, could not afford to fail as a colonized subject and despised *Josenjing,* lower-class status in the Japanese controlled empire. As Park could not afford to fail, he could not trust anyone in his circle of friends, classmates, cadets and fellow army officers until proven trustworthy. This attitude helped him to screen associates and core members of the revolution committee charged with making the revolutionary plan. Park's experience as military intelligence officer gave him an edge in understanding the nature of high-ranking generals in important positions and the capital's, Seoul's security plan.

The revolutionary detail plan was executed not in perfect conditions because of the plan leak and the belated General Chang's, army chief of staff's, order to arrest junta plotters. Nevertheless, the lightning speed and attention to detail helped to avoid potential disaster of armed confrontation between the revolutionary forces, a mere 0.5% of the total troop strength of the nation. Providence must have been working in favor of the historic revolutionary effort as people saw the unmistakable intervention of Providence from the whole picture of the revolution that came to be out in the open. Integration of all relevant facts of the revolution became clear after the 5.16 was complete. Yet, the complex and muddy reality of the revolution movement created much anxiety and suspense.

Many relevant and crucial conditions helping the revolutionary causes surfaced. First, the Second Republic, hurriedly organized after the student revolution on April 19, 1960, was inept and chaotic because the party in power was helplessly mired in internal factional fighting between the two main segments of the ruling party. One was represented by the president, Yoon Bo-sun, and the other premier Chang Myun, who had the authority and power for governing according to the new parliamentary constitution. Nevertheless, Chang was elected by an extremely small margin of votes, just two or three votes, making his cabinet unstable and in constant flux.

Even though both political leaders were from the same party, and they were at the apex of their political careers, they did not have courageous determination to change the old order of corruption and punish the criminal gangs for election-rigging, bribe-taking and violent demonstrations. These elder politicians were naive, face-saving and theoretical without wetting their feet in the reality of living in the poorest country in the world and even a divided country with a constant communist threat. The economy nosedived since the inauguration of the Second Republic with tremendous hope for change and improvements. Unemployment went up 23%, shortage of rice with the increase of price 60%, and the crime rate increased drastically, doubling between December 1960 and April 1961.

Besides, the purge of the previous Liberal Party remnants made the government operation even more ineffective and at a standstill in all branches of government. In addition, the old crimes of election rigging, political use of street gangs, and the killing of 138 students and other demonstrators were not punished by the new government. Bickering in the government continued and the punishment of old crimes through systematic change did not happen and the people's wish for a law-and-order society was lost. As a consequence, the second republic provided an ample justification for the military revolution to happen. On top of this was a major problem which the general public perceived. The national safety apparatus responsible for detecting and destroying organized rebellions, especially in the military, was not functioning well to give advance warning to the national political and military leaders, resulting in enabling the revolutionary plan to continue and be fruitful.

The second factor of the succinct integration of events for the successful 5.16 Revolution was the good timing of the launch of the revolution. The original date for the military action was May 8th, 1960, called The 5.8 Plan. The plan was formulated to remove Syngman Rhee after seeing his old age being manipulated and abused by a curtain of corrupt politicians. President Rhee was eighty-five then and he had had a physically as well as emotionally draining time because of all the work necessary for founding the new Republic of Korea and surviving the brutal Korean War. Fifteen years of hard toil without relief took a heavy toll for the first president Rhee and he failed to screen his close associates and government officials for wanton corruption and election-rigging.

Rhee had been at the center of the chaotic Korean peninsula after his return from long exile in the U.S. for forty years when the Southern half of the Korean peninsula was engulfed in the push and pull with the Soviet-backed communists in the north. It took South Korea under Rhee's leadership to establish a free democracy and a market-based economy in the midst of violent demonstrations, assassination and extreme poverty. Furthermore, he had to manage and survive the brutal fratricidal war within two years of nationhood.

President Rhee negotiated the armistice with the communist north and started recovery of the nation from ashes in his senior years well past the age of retirement. Rhee did not see that his second man and close associate, Lee Ki-boog, and his ambitious wife Park Maria, were in deep corruption and political suicide by engaging in the election-rigging along with Liberal Party functionaries. Lee Ki-boong was in ill health and invalid but his political cronies of the ruling Liberal Party were on their way to wreck the country by enriching their personal wealth through corruption and nepotism. Lee's compulsively ambitious wife and corrupt party officials had a field day influencing all government offices for their get-rich-quick schemes and criminal network-building using their political ties with president Rhee. The ambitious wife of Lee, when Lee was serving as the Liberal Party Chairman, was power hungry. She had two political goals, the immediate goal was her husband's vice presidency with old Syngman Rhee and her long-term goal was the eventual presidency with full intentions to manipulate the old man, Rhee.

President Syngman Rhee, isolated and manipulated by Lee's gang of expedient and clever Liberal Party members, was self-deluded that he was indispensable for the country's recovery and lost a chance for the peaceful and organized transfer of power. This situation led to the student revolution on April 19, 1960. If the military coup was launched while president Rhee was in power, the success of Park's revolution had no guarantee because the courageous strong-willed Rhee could have taken a strong measure to crush the armed rebellion of Park whose death sentence he had commuted. Rhee had unquestionable respect and loyalty from General Song Yo-chan, the Army Chief of Staff, who served as the martial law commander at the time of the student revolution.

Another piece of the integration for the successful revolution was the incredulous attitude of General Chang Do-yong, the new Army Chief of Staff. Ambivalent was the right word to describe General Chang's involvement in the beginning of the revolution, one foot in and one foot out, giving an alibi for either situation. It was a brilliant move on the part of Park Chung-hee to have General Chang connected with the revolution. That connection, factual or illusive, provided the complete justification for the revolutionary movement and a chance to get the support from the entire army. Less than full commitment from General Chang was first viewed as a failure rather than as a success. But in hindsight, Chang's late rather than early involvement was a blessing and not a curse for the success of the revolution.

First, General Chang's name alone carried immeasurable weight plus a certain acknowledgment of the need for the revolution movement from the higher powers in government. Second, General Chang's ambivalence worked well to the revolutionary planners, as a rigid idea from the current army chief of staff could be a possible restriction to open the revolutionary ideas within the trusted group. Ambivalence gave flexibility in discussing revolution strategy among participants without restricting it to one rigid idea from the chief. Leaking crucial information through the channel of the existing army command was risky at best. General Chang was an essential person for the success of the revolution but the farther he was from the revolutionary source, the better to reduce potential leaks of the plan. General Chang's ambivalence helped the initial revolutionary planning by making it fuzzy and less detectable by the national security command.

As General Park recognized the supreme importance of floating General Chang's name as a part of the revolution, Park maintained direct and indirect contact with General Chang continuously concerning the general plan of the revolution but not the details for worry of leak and even betrayal. For instance, as the revolutionary planning proceeded, Park had a private secret meeting with Major General Lee Chu-Il, an old friend and a confidante, to involve

General Chang in the Revolutionary plan. Park agreed when General Lee recommended General Chang as the head of the revolution when the revolution was launched to garner the support of the entire army which would be absolutely necessary for quick consolidation. The piece of General Chang Do-yong was the centerpiece of the puzzle and it had to find its integration into the overall plan.

Yet another piece of integration was the reformist mid-level army officers with staff positions reformed by the urge of their classmates in the revolutionary committee. They formed revolutionary cells in the key army units and divisions near Seoul and the 1st Army. They could observe anti-revolutionary forces and block if necessary during the crucial, initial stages of the revolution. For instance, Major General Lee Han-lim, the Commanding General of the 1st Army with the first defense responsibility against North Korea, was the influential general opposing the military revolution. However, he was quickly neutralized by the revolutionary cell in command within two days of the revolution. He was arrested and brought to Seoul and was kept from the 1st Army. However, Park respected his old Japan Military Academy alumni General Lee for his honesty and straightforward soldier-like attitude and helped him to be productive as head of a civilian– government corporation, a joint venture operation for marine development.

The integration of all pieces for the revolution worked well. As the revolutionary forces occupied all major branch offices of the government, announcement of the pledge of the revolution was repeated at all major functions. An unexpected piece of the puzzle occurred with big fanfare on the main thoroughfare in Seoul. It was the march of the Korean Military Academy Cadets. Again, the effect was electric in gaining national and international attention to the bloodless revolution in progress. Captain Chun Du-whan first recognized the need of support by Korean Military Academy Cadets and recommended it to General Park and junta core members for their immediate approval. Captain Chun was the regular first class Korean Military Academy graduate and was an ROTC instructor at the time. With his gallant and prompt attention to the needs of the revolution to gain recognition by the whole army and the nation, Chun gained access to the Revolutionary Inner Circle for important assignment in the army. Eventually, Chun became the head of the new military command to take over the government aftermath of the assassination of president Park by Kim Jae-gue, KCIA chief. Chun became the president to launch the fifth republic following Park Chung-hee's eighteen year rule to usher South Korea to the rank of a developed country.

Going back to the initial stage of the bloodless revolution, General Park, the second tier military leader, became the supreme power base but General Chang Do-yong was appointed to be the helm of the revolution including Chairman of the Supreme Council of national reconstruction, head of the cabinet, defense minister, and army chief of staff concurrently. But the real power was General Park calling the shots. Proclamations of the revolutionary government including the pledge of revolution went out in General Chang's name. To consolidate national support for the revolution, the pledge of the revolution was repeated at all major government functions throughout the country. The pledge listed six items as objectives: the maintenance of anti-communism, strong ties with the U.S., cleanup of corruption, national economic development, strengthening national power for unification, and lastly going back to original duties after transferring the power.

For the general populace, General Park Chung-hee was mostly unknown and his past was ubiquitous due to his membership in the communist South Korean Workers party. The pledge cleared all the doubts about his allegiance and the big question was how the revolution would revamp the extremely poor national economy. Throughout the Joseon Dynasty, factionalism was a big problem for the division of people and all the subtle or violent infighting among divided factions. For the 5.16 military Revolution, Park and the core members used the factionalism deeply entrenched in the military with fierce competition and strong bonds within the faction. The factions in the Korean military travelled along three lines- types of training, regional divide, and graduation years. Types of training pertains to two obvious sources, Japanese militarism and the U.S. technology and system. Regionality pertains to the background of Manchuria, Korea or Japan where the person was trained and at work. Even for the same military institution, the graduation year of alumnus was enough reason for unity as Kim Jong-pil's class showed.

These factions provided a direct solarium for growth of the plant called military revolution. Revolutionary ideas with similar views of justice and equality, free democracy and economic reconstruction came to grab the members of the Military Revolutionary Committee. Park Chung-hee as the head of the revolution was uncommon in his qualifications to bridge and make a coalition for the greater objective of their country's security and economic prosperity. They had a plan for the new nation with enormous problems of extreme poverty and national security.

Park Chung-hee was monumentally successful to form unity between senior and junior officers, the military people belonging to different factions for the same distilled goal of saving the country.

The team was ready.

16 May 1961 Coup

Park as a South Korean
brigadier general in 1957

Park Chung-hee and
5.16 Military Coup

Seoul, 2013

Seoul, 1961

Park and wife, Yuk Young-soo

Park and daughter,
Park Geun-hye 1960

Park as farmer

Park at POSCO

4.19 Student revolution 1960

Park image

Prince Ito and Crown Prince of Korea

Stalin's photo hung with Kim Il-sung in dreaded communist
Security stations after invasion of South Korea

Kim Il-sung's photo hung with Stalin

Emperor Kojong of
Joseon dynasty of Korea

Park Geun hye defends father's coup

Work and steps for industrialization

SEATO congress

Park with Johnson

President Park geun hye with Obama

9

LET'S GO!

"And to achieve their goal, we have to sweep out dust "

Drastic consequences require drastic measures as in the case of waging war or a revolution.

At the critical moment, the man at the top of the team has to order a command, a command that galvanizes the efforts of the totally dedicated team risking their lives for success. "Let's go." was what Park Chung-hee commanded at pitch dark on May 16th, 1961. The time was 3:00 A.M.

In the early morning of May 16th 1961, the D-day of the planned Revolution, the military security command sent MPs to arrest the ring leaders of the revolution at the order of the army chief of staff, general Chang Do-yong, a definite reversal of events, but Park quickly and courageously made an on-the-spot adjustment and went to the 6th Army District HQ for the historic launch of the revolution. Park had a short but effective troop message for waiting officers and soldiers ready to depart in 2 and 1/2 ton military transports with the unit commander in the military jeep at the very front of the convoy:

We have been waiting for the civilian government to bring back order to the country. The Prime Minister and Ministers, however, are mired in corruption, leading the country to the verge of collapse. We shall rise up against the government to save the country. We can accomplish our goals without bloodshed. Let us join in this Revolutionary Army to save the country.

—Park Chung-hee

This short address was from a general in charge of the revolution, a self-disciplined and self-assured leader who was accustomed to crisis, and it showed the man, the character and something different from opportunistic corrupt politicians deeply factionalized and self-interested. The message was terse and to the point without pretty words. The message was from the heart and delivered in sincerity and military matter-of-factness. The speech was moving and dramatic when the soldiers listened to it in the wee hours before dawn and were ready to move out. The MPs who came to arrest revolutionary officers were moved and joined the revolution by changing their allegiance after listening to the message and became a convincing part of the revolution ready to move.

On May 16, 1961, less than a month after the first anniversary of the student revolution and the second republic under Yoon Bo-sun as president and Chang Myun as Prime Minister, a coordinated military action started. In the pitch-dark night, at 3:00 AM, the crack airborne units with full battle gear assembled on the ground briefly before they boarded trucks in quiet order to occupy Seoul, the capital. They were informed of their mission only a couple of hours before because of the security concern. The long fleet of army trucks with their commander in the very first jeep left the compound. At the commanding general's direct order, the bullets, small arms and automatic rifles were issued to the soldiers eager to change the nation for the better. The convoy of vehicles and soldiers proceeded at the pre-ordered speed and followed the commander's jeep in the front. The dark, tanned faces of soldiers and officers showed the result of long hard training of parachuting and physical fitness to tackle any military assignment at a moment's notice. These troops were the cream of the crop of the army and they enjoyed somewhat elevated respect for their alertness and bravery as they risked their lives every time they jumped from the military transport carrying them to the place of mission.

The crack troops crossed the Han River Bridge, the only bridge spanning over the river, to enter the heart of Seoul, the capital and seat of the government offices. The revolutionary committee's safeguarding of the secret of the impending revolution and the troop assault plan worked well. The advancing troops did not see any sizable defense force blocking their advancement except a small contingent of MPs guarding the normal traffic entering the capital.

The revolutionary truck convoy was not normal traffic but a formidable force to the MP guards. The advancing revolutionary troops quickly overwhelmed the guards and promptly proceeded to the government office centers, the national broadcasting station and the Prime Minister Chang Myun's residence.

Under Park's leadership, the military revolutionary committee worked to gain collaboration and tacit approval of the revolution from the Army Chief of Staff, Chang Do-yong, in secret but not all that hidden in the annals of the intelligence community. General Chang had information on the nature of the revolutionary plot by young officers in the army who had been warned for their open resistance to the military hierarchy for corruption. Chang, though, did not have accurate information on the real nature of the size, the schedule, and troop movements involved in the early-morning rapid action. Chang confused the real massive revolutionary troop movement and took it for the young officer's action of complaint and not real organized revolution. When Chang received reports on the troop movement, he took it as other military maneuvers discussed earlier in preparation for potential violent demonstrations around the first anniversary of the April 19 student revolution. He lost key moments for decisive action to thwart the revolution. Chang knew about the rumors of *coup d'état* and did not make any firm stand either to approve or reject the planned *coup d'état*.

General Chang was not in nor out in the revolutionary plot in the confusion. In a way Chang was mired in the elaborate scheme of confusion devised by Park and his masterminds to blunt the initial shock realized by General Chang or anti-revolutionary forces. Due to the confusion, the revolution forces attained more momentum. speeding up the advance and occupation of major government and mass media facilities without facing much organized resistance. The person in charge of the government, Chang Myun, simply disappeared, hiding in the Catholic nuns' dormitory, losing the critical moment to organize any breakup of the coup attempt. In a mere few hours of the *coup d'état* attempt, the central broadcasting facility in downtown was occupied by the revolutionary forces and they started their blaring broadcasting of the pledge of the revolution.

The pledge was short and itemized to show the objective of the revolution for easy comprehension. The pledge hammered away at the major points the nation and the people were most concerned about, quite effectively drawing more support for the revolution. The revolution quickly galvanized the support of not actively participating military commanders and people quickly watched the uniformed Military Academy cadets parade. The parade had a strong propaganda effect. The revolution received acceptance from the Kennedy administration, paving the way to improve relationships with the strong ally the U.S. and to start the long road to build the economy and clean up the political corruption. The opposing military commanders like Lee Han-rim were arrested and removed from their positions, but were soon reassigned to other important civilian government posts, as Park respected his old comrades and restored them, preferring pacification as a policy for old military associates.

The initial size of the revolutionary forces was approximately 3,600 men out of over 600,000 armed forces, the tip of the iceberg. The size of the force was not enough to bring a crushing blow for the change of the path of the nation. Insufficient army forces caused miraculous results and sweeping changes for important political, military and national matters. The success of the revolution showed the brilliance and determination of the organizers and intervention of Providence, as the revolution was bloodless. Park and his inner circle's ingenuity in masterminding the historical event were noteworthy for their secret planning without a major leak to potential game-changers in the armed forces. The confusion that the revolution committee created in the minds of the army brass was simply outstanding by their combined approach of active and passive tactics. Active tactics refer to the ironclad keeping of the revolutionary plan within the core until the very last minute, and the passive ones were purposeful leaks of confusing information and creating the appearance of the Army Chief of Staff's, General Chang Do-yong's, involvement in the coup.

Originally, the D-Day of the revolution was set on April 19, 1960, the first anniversary of the student uprising, to use the event's distraction for a camouflage for the surprise operation. The date was not kept because an army intelligence unit picked up the trace and there was immediate danger of the entire plan being leaked and investigated. Park had a visitor, an army general in charge of the MP corps, and Park tried to earn more time by confronting the general with moral beseechment and threat of repercussion as well. Park and junior members came to know other bad news in addition to the army intelligence unit on their trail. The bad news was Park was scheduled to be out of active service in May.

Once in the reserves army, Park and the revolution planners thought it would be the end of the revolution plan because without an active leader at the helm of the precarious organization, the assembly of revolutionary forces, secret communication network and logistics of troop movement would be next to impossible. Already certain coup members worried about abortion of the revolution as the resistance force would be formed when the army chain of command came to know the military revolutionary committee and its organization and plan.

The power cord must be pulled and the revolution members had to find their own light and power while Park was in the active army position with the general's insignia to unite the rebel forces for a "do-or-die" implementation of the revolutionary plot. The new final date for the revolution was set for May 16, 1961, with firm determination to carry it out in less than a month past the 1st anniversary of the April 19th student uprising. In the development of the first wave of the armed forces' speedy move to Seoul, the Army Airborne units were selected as the main thrust for their gung-ho spirit and ease of control as the unit had a separate base and independent command structures. The airborne unit with their unique battle fatigues and bony and muscular soldiers advanced to their pre-assigned government facilities in the highly coordinated military operation.

They occupied the assigned offices and arrested people on their list to quell any resistance effort. The first wave also made arrangements to mobilize the reserve army division if necessary by key staff officers already in the plot or by their forcible demand to the shocked division commanders of regions without direct involvement in the revolutionary matters. The committed staff in the divisional command was deeply involved through the Military Academy class association with Kim Jong-pil at the center, a direct link to Park Chung-hee, the mastermind of the revolution. The division commander did not have much choice on gunpoint negotiation and demand for support for the revolutionary cause. Full tank battalions were mobilized for their show of strength and parked outside the city limit.

The first assault plan of the troop convoy of the revolutionary force was lightning occupation and safeguard of critical government and mass media facilities in the capital and then the arrest of key government leaders that included the president, Yoon Bo-sun, the Prime Minister, Chang Myun, the cabinet members, and the Supreme Court chief judge. The second thrust was to force divisions of the 1st Army responsible for the defense of the nation from the communist North to stay put where they were and not mobilize. The critical reasoning for the action was to remove any possibility of civil war between the revolutionary forces and government forces. Beyond that, the goal was to remove the concern of national defense as the communist North might try to find a defense gap created by the revolutionary troop movements and people's acceptance of the current changes. As long as the 1st Army kept its position and stayed intact, it was like hitting two birds with one stone, consolidation of revolutionary forces and the national defense from the North.

The staff of the front line divisions were already posted by revolutionary officers either by their being part of the plot or being pledged not to go against the revolution. The entire division of the 1st Army commanders were quickly identified and evaluated for their loyalty. If they were anti-revolution, they were arrested by the negotiation officers dispatched from the central revolution steering committee neutralizing any anti-revolution effort. The trenches dug by revolutionary forces along the outer city limits for potential armed confrontation were unnecessary to dispel the worries of revolution leaders. Luckily, most division commanders were quickly convinced of the swift success of the revolutionary agenda to overturn the current government.

The capsizing and removal of the grossly ineffective Second Republic by force was swift as the responsible ran away or went into hiding. As soon as the army of revolution was in control of Seoul, the capital and government offices, Park and the revolution leaders tried to sway General Chang Do-yong, the chief of staff, to the side of the revolution to consolidate their position and to start the long road of reconstruction. By making General Chang an integral part of the revolution, the revolutionary committee was certain that legitimacy of the revolution was firmly established to calm doubters and resistors of the historical event taking place, especially when the sitting President Yoon had quickly supported the revolution within days of the military coup d'etat.

General Chang's position was not clear before and immediately after the coup, but to unify the forces of the revolution, Chang was useful as the face of the revolution. General Chang's cooperation was good to have but required no begging from Park and revolution leaders as the revolution was a fait' accompli and was destined for success. Already, during the initial occupation of the Korean Army headquarters in Sam Gag Ji, Seoul, General Chang had unscrupulous visits from pistol-yielding revolution members openly demanding his support or else. "Or else" meant obvious fall from his position and power. A real force of the revolution, Park and his immediate members took the second row of power with full control to make room for the Army Chief of Staff Chang. Chang was swayed and became the center of attention by holding the most powerful positions in the nation at the time: chairman of the Supreme Council of national reconstruction, the Prime Minster and the defense minister positions concurrently.

Despite the fact that Chang held all the powerful positions, it was questionable if he was the powerful leader of the revolution as history revealed in just a few months. Chang supplied the credibility the revolution committee and the course of revolution required for nationwide approval and support for the reconstruction of the nation. General Chang in his uniform with four stars and talking in staccato soon filled the media in on matters regarding the revolutionary council for national reconstruction. Chang performed his duty well as the face of the revolutionary effort but it appeared he did not command real power and did not have his key men in the Revolutionary Council, creating an insecure power position without real backbone. Chang lacked the nerve and determination either to stop and crush the revolution or to be a bona fide real power behind the revolution as the handpicked Army Chief of Staff by the inept Second Republic. The two-star general Park behind the revolution had more risk with firm conviction than the four-star general Chang with more power position to protect as a part of the Second Republic. The results were clear and convincing for both generals.

As the revolutionary effort took root and was secured for success, the reorganization of governing functions for national reconstruction quickened in all branches of government: the legislative branch, the court, and the executive offices, under scrutiny of the revolutionary Council. In the whirlwind of the reconstruction effort, Chairman Chang knew that pendulum-style commitment once for the inept Second Republic and now for the revolution might not sit well and put him in trouble. The reconstruction effort would require real, courageous, result-oriented tasks, as it dealt with people and bureaucrats with a long ingrained monarchic and colonial mentality.

Even though Chang had a higher rank and a powerful position in the army with unwavering support from the then-civilian government being headed by premier Chang Myun, he was not a match for Park in handling military intelligence, crisis analysis and resolution, and decisive and daring problem solving with or without force. Park's years of military training in the world-renowned Imperial Japan military academies and his survival instinct gave him uncanny talents for problem resolution, whether it was political infighting or military preparedness in times of real problem.

At the first signs of bickering and rumor of assassination of Park from Chang's camp, Chang was quickly arrested on charges of anti-revolution and an assassination attempt and removed from all powers and visibility. Chang's grab of national power as part of Park's strategy did not last more than a couple of months. Park and the loyal revolutionary council members took over all the posts Chang and his close associates held. The real force of the revolution was firmly entrenched, strengthened, and stayed unquestionably with Park and his loyal supporters. They realized the value of Chang as the face of the revolution was over as the dynamic plan of the revolution was steadfastly implemented. The supreme council methodically removed a potential blocking force and anti-revolution forces to fulfill the pledged objectives of the revolution, by first establishing KCIA (Korean Central Intelligence Agency) with Kim Jong-pil as its first head. KCIA was to control and remove any potential forces in the way of the national reconstruction and any subversive groups with communist ties.

Chang Do-yong's removal was complete when he was led away in handcuffs and in customary old-fashioned white baggy Korean trousers comfortable for prison life. The media coverage of Chang's arrest was a sort of warning to other military elements pondering organizing an anti-revolutionary act rather than physical punishment, as seen by Chang's release a short time after and his travel to the U.S. for a renewed quiet life. Consolidating revolutionary forces also quickened changes in political and social life for the better. Many old political criminals responsible for the massive election fraud causing students' uprisings and casualties had not been brought to justice. Now they were before the military court for hearing and sentencing. The street gangs organized and used for political purposes, including election ballot changes, intimidation of voters, and other lawless anti-social activities, were rounded up by the same airborne units and forced to parade on the downtown streets of Seoul with placards identifying their names and organizations. The quick action to bring criminals and violent gangs to justice gave a long sigh of relief to anxiously waiting citizens. Nationwide approval and support for the revolution soon followed with added speed and strength.

Park resumed the chairmanship of the Supreme Council of national reconstruction and garnered the control of the most powerful interim military government, mapping the next significant move to unify forces in government and the military for the immediate task of drafting the five-year economic development plan and funding the plan.

Park and other council members started appearing in casual volleyball games right in the government office compound on the conspicuous Se Jong Ro clad in running shirts and shouting for game points. The look of young energetic and physically fit military officers in the tough demanding work of national reconstruction was moving and encouraging to the public. Tanned, slender and physically fit Supreme Council members showed a clear departure from the scene of the old political figures with their clumsy physiques and authoritative Yang Ban (noble class) appearance. The remnant of the old monarchic and colonial attitude, division of classes and the ruling by personality had not vanished. The fierce factional strife and myopic self-interest and nepotism persisted dangerously in the Second Republic. The poverty, high unemployment and the hopeless condition looked insurmountable and the defeatism permeated every area of the society. Deep surgical operation and comprehensive reconstruction efforts were a must, not a choice.

The shameful title of the poorest country in the world with a mere $87 GDP per capita and the deplorable shortage of rice and food put young children in the classroom and on the playground playing soccer games with empty stomachs. When Park and the Supreme Council members looked over the government operation, they knew they had walked into a hornet's nest with chronic problems of poverty, denuding of the once-green mountains, and massive corruption in every level of society. The opening of the empty coffer of the national treasury and the files of various social and monetary problems gave nothing but shock and disappointment as the nation was on the brink of bankruptcy with the patient on his death bed with only with a few breaths left.

Park and the revolution members were ready to die for the revolutionary cause when they started the revolution, but now they realized clearly that not even sacrifice of one's life was enough to tackle the undaunting problem without money, credit in international commerce, and no natural resources to tap. Where could they find money to start the ambitious plan of revolution for the two objectives: elimination of tearing poverty and self-defense of the country from the communists? In a poorly conceived measure for immediate money flow, the revolutionary government launched the feared currency change from "hwan" to "won" with a different set value and dollar exchange rate in the hope of catching the hidden money. Currency change did not catch hidden money as the entire nation was poor.

The government economic planner thought that a big part of circulating money was hidden by Chaebol, the big family owned companies, former corrupted government officials and even Chinese immigrants doing their big restaurant and import businesses in secret and in ways hard to account for. The result of the currency change was nothing but failure and disappointment. The country did not have many rich people or businesses with money. The market economy Syngman Rhee instilled worked well not only in distribution of wealth but also the spread of real poverty that continued for generations. The ambitious revolutionary government had to scramble for another funding source. In the meantime, symbolic changes to set a new course for the nation were announced including the youngest member of the Supreme Council to chair in case of the chairman's dysfunction, a departure from age-old blind respect of old people. In more drastic measures to change the old tradition of isolation, the calendar used for a millennium was changed suddenly from the Korean calendar of five thousand years to the Western calendar to align the nation's compatibility with the other developed nations for commerce and trade.

Inconvenience in changing stationary, birth years and other

historical references was negligible in comparison to the hope and optimism to become a modern and developed country where people would enjoy freedom and economic self-sufficiency without worrying about watching young children running around with empty stomachs. Visible energy and optimism were noticeable but that did not guarantee a meal ticket. Without money and without capital, even powerful revolutionary government could not do much to feed hungry people and invigorate the deteriorating environment without clean water, decent housing, and safe and efficient social, education and transportation infrastructures.

When there was no money, no capital inside of the country, the leaders of the Supreme Council had to look elsewhere for capital to start the planned Economic Development. Time was running out and extreme measures were on the horizon. The nation in a mess had to find an immediate funding source but without readily available alternatives. Only two areas presented any hope: one was negotiation of blood money Japan owed to Korea for its thirty-six years of colonization and trampling of Korean assets, the other was the potential export of unemployed but well-educated and willing men and women.

As the new administration looked for foreign loans, even with a higher interest rate, to jumpstart the nation's economy and manufacturing, the government effort met with a constant negative response from foreign banking systems, with the excuse that Korea had no acceptable credit rating for any loan either from foreign governments or private banking institutions. This was a chicken and egg situation, propelling the vicious circle of poverty. Park Chung-hee, as the head of the new administration, was willing to do anything to get a breakthrough. He first tried the ally, the U.S., and the International Monetary Fund for loans, without any success. The only thing he could see was the backs of powerful people. Park believed the old adage he lived by that stated, "Where there is a will, there is a way." Also he understood the common wisdom that men in the fox hole best know the soldiers' predicament. Similar hardship leads to understanding. Park wanted to contact West Germany for help since both Germany and Korea had the heart-wrenching pain of wisdom, both went through the destruction of great wars and division of the country, and both countries wanted to reconstruct from total ruins.

Nevertheless, Germany was much more ahead in economic recovery than South Korea and Korea wanted to emulate Germany as the success model for industrialization. Park started a rigorous and high-level contact for a possible summit meeting to discuss a potential economic assistance program for poverty-stricken Korea. Soon, Germany hired Korean nurses and miners for their labor shortage in their expanded economy and also gave the Korean government a loan using the wages of Korean workers as the collateral. The summit meeting with high expectations from Koreans took place when Park and his entourage reserved a space in a German commercial airplane and made the state visit. The Korean government was so poor that a presidential plane, Air Force One, was not a possibility. The summit meeting was highly successful for mutual understanding of Korea's need for economic development and Germany's hire of Korean labor for mutual benefit. Koreans needed the wages and Germany needed expatriate workers for their expanding economy.

Besides the monetary assistance, Park learned important economic development lessons, including Germany's construction of expressways and dynamically-staged industrialization with emphasis on the export economy. Then, another emotional meeting followed between Park, his wife Yuk Young-soo and the Korean workers in Germany, mostly nurses and miners working hard labor a few thousand miles away and separated from their families. The event turned into a weeping and crying public gathering when all stood and sang the Korean national anthem. Park's prepared speech before the group quickly dropped from his hands and a white handkerchief with the stain of tears was in his hand instead. The meeting was a sober reminder of the precarious situation of the country for both the leader and expatriate workers. The nation and the people could not afford to lose any momentum and energy from overcoming chronic poverty through vigorous economic development and industrialization. It was a rare moment, for the nation's leader and common people saw their problems and solutions in a united and determined way.

The on-again, off-again negotiations for normalizing the relationship between Japan and Korea had not seen the light at the end of the tunnel for nearly two decades since liberation in 1945. The gully was still deep and unfathomable between the two countries and the painful track could not be erased after the long thirty-six years of brutal colonization that trampled both Korean material wealth and mental assets. Yet, normalizing the relationship was important and crucial for Korean economic development, the peace, and future defense against communism in the region. For Japan, the superior and lucrative position was not diminished owing to the Korean War that enriched them with their blistering business for war material supplies while Korea was reduced to a heap of rubles. Japan did not want to rush through the negotiation for compensation and the Korean government under Syngman Rhee did not wish to open the normalizing talk from an inferior position. Nevertheless, the new country after the military revolution saw the need from a more open mind and practical point of view.

The normalizing talk might go on and off continuously without any plausible gain to both sides. Korea was in a different condition under Park's leadership and his eagerness to develop a country's economy had a certain priority. Korea needed capital and a market for the economic development plan. Korea could demand Japan to pay compensation for Japanese colonial trampling at a price that could be a stumbling block. Demand and willingness to pay had a large gap. For the Korean side, time was crucial and more recompensation by waiting longer years might not produce better results. The patient needed the medicine immediately and waiting might not be an option. Park, a patriotic and practical man, had formed from his upbringing and hard military training the wisdom to know that a bird in the hand is worth two in the bush.

He decided to quicken the normalization to get the precious capital to fund the planned Economic Development and to develop a market for Korean products to be exported to Japan to have better balance. At the time, Korean imports were much higher than exports but with normalization, the scales would be more balanced. The normalization talks went through with mutual agreement but it was completed too quickly for large segments of the Korean population and anti-negotiation demonstrations followed for some time. Yet, the old agreement on normalization became a fact, helping commercial activities between the two countries and Korea bought more industrial machinery from Japan to head-start manufacturing for more exports. The target was simple products like wigs, toys, and related merchandise first and then hi-tech items likes electronics and chemicals later. From negotiated loans, wages from West Germany and the compensation and loans from Japan, Park's government had the necessary funds required for the development plan.

Park was thankful and made it abundantly clear that the blood money would be used in the most effective and honest way to speedily reconstruct the nation. The government had the necessary capital which was not enough to squander and the leader and technocrats in charge of national reconstruction had an additional obligation to watch the capital use. Capital could not be siphoned as in other nations to line pockets of corrupt politicians or spent on luxury items for people in power such as golf courses or resort facilities. The hard-gained capital might bring about an Industrialization Age for the nation dreaming of enough rice and food for its people. If achieved, that would be a historical change, paving the way for full industrialization and higher national standing in the world, from poorest nation to aid-giving nation with eventual reunification of the Korean peninsula with that economic and self defense capability. History would tell about Park's leadership and the Supreme Council's effort for the national reconstruction.

What would history tell?

With the luxury of hindsight that provides a perfect mirror to reflect reality, the post generation would not have to go through what-if considerations of the historical event of the 5.16 military Revolution. Every piece of the great puzzle of the bloodless epochal revolution, *coup d'état* or armed rebellion, whatever term the future generation may use, are right here at our fingertips to digest and understand the "why," "what," and "how.". In the five-thousand year history of Korea, the Military Revolution and the leadership Park Chung-hee provided created the most brilliant change of the social, economic and national defense of the country. The clear impact of the brilliant revolution, comparable to Japan's Meiji restoration movement and Singapore's building of its foundation was felt by Koreans but in reality it goes far beyond its borders. The revolution presented to the whole world, especially poor backward countries in Africa, Middle East and elsewhere, a model of self-improvement and economic self-sufficiency in a clear and straightforward manner.

In war, nothing may be spared for winning, so in revolution, as no alternative exists. Change the old order or be destroyed. A revolution is a war and even more dangerous than conventional war because a revolution does not stop at the end of conflict, it starts for new changes. A revolution is a different kind of war where the revolutionary team is fighting against established government and the power base with self-defense, and the recognition of the general populace. Once a war or a revolution starts, the plan is completely useless and quickly thrown out to conduct the necessary affairs to win and build momentum. Park as the mastermind and his team made the painstaking revolutionary plan in secret and rehearsed for a long time in minute detail, but when the troop movement started, they forewent the plan to concentrate on the events rapidly in progress and tried to make adjustments quickly and with a definite sense of direction.

Pistol-yielding revolutionary members were at key places to occupy including the office of the army chief of staff, general Chang Do-yong, in the army headquarters at Samgakji, Seoul, while soldiers were at the ready with rifles and bullets at the entrance of the headquarters, the heart of the armed forces. The previous plans: the 5.8 Plan in 1960 to oust President Rhee, the second 4.19 Plan in 1961, the third 5.12 Plan in 1961 and the final 5.16 Plan in 1961, came and went. Only the final plan succeeded. Each plan had its own merits and limitations but they did not matter, only the plan finally executed mattered.

General Park Chung Hee and his men were ready to die for a cause so that the corrupt politicians and power-hungry "liberation aristocrats" forming the thick and impenetrable curtain around the corrupt and inept power for their own profit would be in check. They were ready to fight to eliminate the extreme poverty, injustice, and chaos in the country in armistice with ever belligerent communists to the north.

In a calm and emotionless voice, the final order of the revolution parted from the lips of general Park Chung-hee.

Let's go!

10

A VILLAGE WITH A NEW ROOF

"What are we going to do with that large group of people who are full of disappointment, despair, hunger, and lethargy?"

A chorus of laughter and joyous shouting with broad grins on their faces came to the family and its neighbors when the old thatched roof of the mud house was replaced with orange colored tiles for the first time in their family history. The positive marshaling of the nation's labor force, the seed money capital, and their ambitious economic plan started to show results when more houses in the rural villages replaced the old thatched roofs with bright orange colored tiles.

What was happening?

The farmers and rural people were surprised to see new more optimistic things happen in their once sleepy villages. They welcomed widening of gravel roads, building of small bridges over ravines, and supply of electricity for the first time in the villages' history. More things came to revolutionize the old sleepy and primitive life. The rural life that depended on tree leaves, stumps, and cut trees for cooking and heating suddenly changed with coal bricks. Generations of this practice to cut trees in close mountains in the back of the villages caused the Green Mountains to be denuded and barren. More trees were cut because of short supply of firewood, making the mountains bare and brown-colored as the trees got scarce. Year after year, collection of wood for heating and cooking became more difficult as more people went to nearby mountains to cut trees. Collection of wood became full-time, all-day work and the people's precious time and labor were unproductive and damaging the land with mudslides and floods. Inconvenient and expensive at first, anthracite coal replaced wood for cooking and heating following the new government policy. Tree-cutting stopped and organized efforts started to plant seedlings to restore the mountain.

The government brought coal to villages from coal mines and tree-cutting was strictly prohibited. At first, the new government policy with heavy penalties wreaked havoc and almost caused a revolt as people could not cook and heat their on-dol bang, the traditional stone slated floor absorbing wood-burning heat underneath. More trucks and sometimes military trucks brought coal on an emergency basis and the people's lifestyles changed to use the coal in the form of a 19-hole circular brick that lasted almost 24 hours, saving effort and energy for other productive use. The many-centuries-old kitchen had to be remodeled to fit the changing reality as the result of the revolution. As soon as the tree-cutting stopped, the new government initiatives started for villages to plant tree saplings on barren soil all over the mountain area to restore the brown mountains once densely wooded and green. People complained for inconvenience and work involved, and yet, as more saplings were planted, more hopes came that they were doing something productive individually and collectively for the future generations.

People first thought that Park and his administration were either ignorant of easy government policy for people or outright dictatorial. No other governments before had tried the green policy in an organized manner with eagerness and intensity to change the old life. Well, the government under Park's leadership was not an ordinary government and the future would tell the causes and effects with ample evidence. With 335 bags of free cement and reinforcing bars supplied to 33,000 villages, people started to replace the old mud walls with blocks, making the houses cool in summer and warm in winter. Treated running water came to houses by a simple piping system and a new drainage system was designed and constructed to modernize old kitchens and toilets for the first time in village life. Village libraries were formed and people started reading and discussing small family business under bright electric light. Soon, radios, TVs and small computers showed up, giving and sharing technical and business information among villagers that was possible only to city dwellers before.

Rural families with much less income started to have small business opportunities like making dolls, wigs, parts of sneakers, clothes, and assembly of small electronic machines to make extra money. Their businesses expanded as the general economy grew strong and government assistance was available for goods and services geared for export. More technical items with higher profit margins came for manufacturing of electronic items, auto parts for overseas after-market, electric gauges and even dried and canned foodstuffs. In fact, Korean-style fried noodles, ramen with hot sauce, became a big export item as many countries all over the world came to like them. Spanish -speaking people in South America and Middle Eastern countries had a special fondness for hot ramen, making its export brisk.

After Park Chung-hee's transformation from the military leader to the civilian political reformer in the spirit of transferring power to the civilian government, the nation saw the establishment of the Third Republic of Korea with a new constitution based on the revolutionary objectives and tenets. The new Republic with Park Chung-hee at the center continued its emphasis and support for the export economy and all-out encouragement was given to export-related small business development. There was unmistakable new zeal and accelerated progress in the national economy. The rural villages had more incentives from the government to improve their villages for modernization of living and living environment. People came to see more improvement in Small Business Systems and modernization, ranging from the roof replacement to remodeling of kitchens, bathrooms and the infrastructure for transportation, education and the decentralized government systems.

The rural and micro-farming villages came to have a new burst of hope, strength and experience for the enhanced economic progress through the small export business. For the first time in Korean history, equality in income and lifestyle came closer with rural annual income growth becoming higher than the cities. With additional family income and cooperative communal work experience, more mechanized and efficient systems came for processing and transporting rural products and the catch of fishing towns. More application of research and development of farming, production and transport came to produce more rice per unit of land. Massive use of vinyl for farming of vegetables revolutionized food production. As a result, a quality and quantity of food became available for ordinary people not seen in Korean history. People did not have to depend on rice alone for predominant nutrition as more delicious and nutritious side dishes of fish and all kinds of vegetables came to the dinner table. Koreans and foreign tourists could not hide their delight when facing the meal table for the taste and variety.

The abundance of food was a real part of the revolutionary objectives and now farmers and poor Koreans did not worry about the anxious period between the harvest of barley and rice as Koreans called it *bo ri go gae*, meaning the barley hill. Barley had a couple of months' earlier harvest than rice in Korea and poor farmers and ordinary people were out of predominant grains before the rice harvest. The barley harvest was a must to survive before the rice. Not anymore, and it was the salient and heartfelt achievement of the revolution. People agreed that it would pave the way for ensuing national reconstruction and entrance to the pact of modernized nations in the world.

Drastic changes started to come when the initial stage of the revolution was complete. As the pledge of the revolution was announced regularly and its commitment propagated in the whole nation and beyond the borders, the support for the revolution grew exponentially with less likelihood of anti-revolutionary forces gathering in and out of the country. Even the Kennedy government nodded on the revolution earlier than expected. The winds of changes started to show on the streets, marketplaces, government offices, and social and political events. The members of the supreme council for national reconstruction were dutifully engaged in all sorts of positive and inspiring events, starting with the visit to the national cemetery of the brave, the patriots and the independence fighters who died for the nation.

People used to the old feudal and colonial rule for generations were passive, dependent and unmotivated to initiate any self or community improvements. They accepted living hand-to-mouth in abject social conditions as their ancestors had lived, under monarchical and colonial rule without much hope. The big disparity in living standards in villages and the major cities with commercial and industrialized concentration was widespread, with people leaving their villages to go to overcrowded cities and repeating the cycle of poverty and no hope. The new 5.16 revolutionary government under Park's leadership spared nothing to jumpstart the new social behavior of "What can we do?" to "We can." Yet, the country had been so poor and so shortsighted, no infrastructure was available for the start of economic development. Gingerly in the military, Park had worked for many years to prepare the basis for industrialization. Park established the economic planning board with an ambitious reconstruction plan to help the nation eventually enter the rank of a developed country.

With no accumulated skills and capital, and no natural resources, the task of economic development was immensely difficult but President Park refused to accept the status quo with firm belief in Korean people's past investment in education and their diligent character to produce when opportunities were available. Park started government-guided economic development starting with small manufacturing first and then continuing to the process of heavy industrialization. He used a small capital loan from West Germany on condition of collateralizing the wages earned by Korean nurses and miners selected for the precious work in Germany. In addition, Park's courageous effort to normalize relations with Japan provided the seed money for Keongbu Expressway, the biggest project in Korean history to open the era of modernization.

Park's training in the top notch Imperial Japan's military academies with militarism and the samurai's spirit of honesty and fearlessness helped him to take on the challenge of the initial economic development. The nation was in a dire situation and he treated it like a war where he used the command "Export!" instead of "Attack!" The government leaders in the economic planning board had to take the national manufacturing and export capability "as is" not "as they hoped." They had to make the most of available resources and opportunity to transform Korea in extreme poverty to self-sufficiency. Park and the economic technocrats were keenly aware of the large disparity between overcrowded big cities and the rural farm villages where more than seventy percent of the population lived. Park and his economic experts needed something, a powerful shot in the vein, for the country. *Saemaul Undong*, the community development movement, was what Park inaugurated as a national policy to answer such disparity.

Nevertheless, *Saemaul Undong* was not his priority because the general economy and the nation's safety against ever-present communist North's threat had to be dealt with first. The first shot of medicine had to go that patient first. When Korea was the poorest country in the world with a per capita income of $87, his priority was irrigation problem was solved, farming became more productive and their grain shortage became manageable.

From this experience of collectively working together with a small loan, villagers came to have more self-confidence and soon had another small project to improve the life at the village with cheap cement and reinforcing iron bars they got from the government relief agency. More projects followed to widen the village dirt road and the building of a small culvert to bridge a small stream. Now, villagers were talking about replacing the old traditional thatched roofs with something else and their attention went to their toilets and cooking area.

The village changed because of one active leader in the village with common sense and motivation. The transformation was electric, from abject poverty and helplessness to a functional community with hope and more projects to do. The village became the model for *Saemaul Undong*, rural community development. Nearby villages saw the direct benefits of self-help and communal work with the same objective and soon followed the government guide to obtain free cement and free iron bars for their projects without going through time-consuming and painful red tape or bribing.

Starting with what the people in rural areas could do to reforest the denuded village hills and mountains, Park initiated a systematic approach for the self-help program and narrowed the economic and social gap between rural and urban living. From the start, Park did not believe in giving away construction material, cement and steel the country could make available unless the project had a leader and a plan to produce the desired result. The official inauguration of *Saemaul Undong* was on April 22, 1970 as a way to modernize the country with a nest egg and chosen collaborating villages as partners.

The essential components of the movement applied the government policy as a driving force and consisted of a few salient parts: the engaged people, the seed money, the guiding principle and the movement leader. As in any organization or group project, the leader would have a critical role to make the movement successful. The leader might not possess the higher education or experience, but should be a person with common sense and the drive to inspire other people to finish what they started. The government agencies involved in projects used the qualification of the project leader as the important criteria to award or reject the project.

completed the projects on time or in advance of the original schedule. When people saw the tangible result showing a completely different and modernized look for the village from thatched roofs to colorful roof tiles, the *Saemaul Undong* spread to other villages like a forest fire. More individual and community improvements followed in accelerated speed.

The living standard was raised and the family income rose, and in the process, the poor villagers saw the transformation in themselves from poor defeated people to the middle-class. The middle-class, or the backbone of democracy, now had resources to expand the village hall to annex a small library where they read, learned and practiced new computer games while their awareness of free democracy and its operations enhanced. These people participating in *Saemaul Undong* were late bloomers and they behaved with utmost eagerness and determination to learn from their books at the village library about new small business and town politics.

They started to debate at the village meetings, driving off the timid and passive attitude they had before. Some wise village elders worried about the young villagers with new enthusiasm and eagerness without sufficiently long practice as a democratic citizenry. They worried they could become a curse rather than a blessing for the country. Somewhat extreme people might become victims of propaganda and socialistic utopian barrage from the communists and their sympathizers in South Korea. People leaning towards socialism or communism in developing democracy tended to complain for complaint's sake, especially when they saw gaps between the rich and the poor. The ignorance of socialist activists prevented them from seeing the majority good. The activists misled by communist theory suggested the naïve people look for a perfect solution. They could see only the trees and not the forest that provided so much good for the society.

Some villagers participating in the community movement became selfish zealots insisting on "my home, my village and my interest" first and foremost rather than the national concern to deal with the bigger problem of communism and spies in their midst. Opposition political leaders and left-leaning radicals tried to use the new awakening "middle class", the product of economic progress, for opposition political parties' gain. These unqualified and corrupt politicians of the opposition political parties incited the new middle class to violent demonstrations and riots at the slightest controversy. Unexpected things happened to the surprise of *Saemaul* organizers and Park. The surprise was as people's life improved as the result of *Saemaul Undong*, the people's political support for the government became lesser or reduced. The surprising "reverse effect" was as people entered the middle class, their political awareness went to the underdog or the opposition parties.

In other words, to get more votes from people, *Saemaul Undong* was a laughable failure in vote getting, but the *Undong* was a resounding success to improve people's lives and help them to enter the middle class. It was an irony that less votes meant more success. The new political awareness with a better living standard and without fear of food shortage made people go over the fence to the side of the opposition expecting a more perfect democracy that was somewhat compromised for the nation's reconstruction and industrialization. By helping the backward and poor rural farming areas, Park's government ended up losing some rural votes. With a chuckle, Park accepted the reverse effect as approval of the *Saemaul Undong* and took it as a diploma of the tough course he had taken for the poor and sick nation.

Green mountains and village hills changed their color and look as the result of the nationwide reforestation policy. The elimination of the disparity between rural areas and cities, and a drastic increase of income per capita through "export first" policy were real and factual. The government did not manufacture the historical success by falsifying statistical data on economics. People lived better and gained confidence from the old defeatism to a "we can do" spirit awaiting another challenge of individual and nationwide improvement of democracy and industrialization.

From one most qualified technocrat President Park, the country saw the will and spirit of the people to continue the reconstruction of the nation. Industrialization and the resounding success of *Saemaul Undong* helped the once poorest country in the world enter the ranks of developed countries in the world in less than one generation. That same poor aids-receiving country became, to the heartfelt surprise of the world, an aid-giving country. *Saemaul Undong* spread in force to some seventy-six countries to help the socio-economic development of poor countries in Africa, Asia, and other neglected areas of the world.

Park Chung-hee was at the center of all these patriotic, pragmatic, and technocratic actions of brilliance without enriching himself or his family, a sign of a true hero. Even in remote villages and fishing towns, people began to enjoy enough food, running water, electricity and modern appliances like the middle-class of a developed country. "In a decade, even mountains and rivers change," a common saying, came to carry real meaning to people when they watched the mountains and rolling hills getting greener everyday. When Park Chung-hee saw in his frequent trips to once starving farming villages, a grandmother holding her small grandson, well fed and healthy, walking on the clean village macadam road, his eyes got wet remembering his mother in tearing poverty and malnutrition. Mother always believed he would do something important and significant for their poor country. And now what?

11

INDUSTRIALIZATION COUP WITHIN A COUP

"South Korea is overcrowded, absolutely lacking in resources, but a manufacturing industry hardly exists."

The confidence to move mountains came when the people and the government had successfully moved small mounds. Now, the long dreamed of industrialization of the nation according to the ambitious successive five-year economic development plan started in 1962 without much fanfare, but with unswerving determination and enormous confidence.

The strong headwinds created by history's unpredictable waves of ups and downs, especially by the Korean War, communism, colonialism, and monarchism, started to turn the headwinds to tailwinds for the continuous achievement of the goals of the Economic Plan. The waves began to subside and people became more hopeful to see the tailwinds by changing the position of the ship called the ROK, Republic of Korea. The ship had been under new leadership represented by the personal conviction and charisma of Park Chung-hee. The stumbling blocks in the way of the nation's industrialization were removed one by one and the momentum had been strong with the new capital infusion from the successful "export-first" policy and continuing preparation for the quantum jump to the planned nation's industrialization.

The blood money was invested under careful and brutal watch of Park's administration with warning of major punishment for any illegal or personal use. The warning was blatant and dictatorial to avoid any corruption and nepotism as had happened many times by corrupt high-level government officials using their power, intimidation, and dishonesty. Park saw other colonized countries compensated by Japan use the money to build mansions for government officeholders. Park did not want this to happen and as in many important military operations, Park led the bayonet charge to corruption, especially handling the blood money attributable to every Korean. Every dollar must go to the national reconstruction and economic progress by helping the export business and possibly building steel mills, heavy chemical plants, and the most modern industrial sites to compete in the world.

For a family living hand to mouth, a sack of rice means safety, security, and self-esteem all combined. An empty sack gives the traumatic feeling of nothing to put on the family table at meal time. For a mother of a large family responsible for preparing meals, the empty sack is an uncontrollable fear and physical torture. To her, mealtime is coming too quick and as the mealtime approaches, the poor mother feels bone-rattling pain and the feeling of utter helplessness. Park as the youngest of six was not an exception to feel the same pain his Mom had at mealtime and deep inside of him, poverty was the #1 enemy to conquer for his family first and eventually for the entire country. Every time Park had to make important decisions that might help economic development, giving enough food to put on the poor farmer's kitchen tray, his mother's image lingered.

Thus, every family and the nation entertained the dream of providing enough food for all, rich and poor. In Korea, the chronic poverty and food shortage persisted for many generations without consistent political leadership to solve the problem and fulfill the basic dream of enough food to eat. Nevertheless, without capital, and resources but many mouths to feed, the government had been at a loss in implementing a long-term economic development plan. The government policy was to bridge the gap of crisis and could not entertain an ambitious plan of self-sufficiency immediately due to the existing limitations. Park and his economic leadership desired to develop the economy as soon as possible but they also knew that they had to take steps one by one and could not jump over many major steps. Like people, the government could not run when they could not even crawl. In a conscious and consistent way, Park had his economic policy developed by the U.S.-trained economists in collaboration with all government agencies, private conglomerates, research institutes, labor organizations and especially banking institutions to get seed money to implement each step of the overall economic plan.

As seed money established through tough foreign loans, credits, and repayment of Korea's claim by Japan for normalizing their relationship, the "export first" policy had first priority to get the money. The policy had been kept up to provide stepping stones for crossing the stream to industrialization. The economic planning board created to formulate policy decisions and benchmark the progress of economic development had enjoyed wholehearted and dedicated support from Park as the progress surpassed the goal of export by industry and even by companies. The seed money for economic development with loans and the hard-negotiated compensation from Japan was blood money for Koreans too precious to squander.

Park made sure every penny of that seed money would go to economic development and he personally checked the progress of the planned economic goals. He would troubleshoot if necessary so that the whole country and government economic policy continued to work in a comprehensive and coordinated manner. Never before had all forces in the nation gathered to achieve one objective, one objective alone, to eliminate chronic poverty. The national drive for the goal was so intensive under Park's revolutionary leadership, major projects like Keongbu Expressway, and the heavy chemical industry, shipbuilding industry, auto manufacturing industry and the defense industry had President Park as their project manager for project execution and delivery.

People educated but underemployed, and poor farmers without enough land were rigorously tapped as major resources to go over the hurdles of the economic challenges. Previous governments long neglected or mismanaged this segment of people due to insufficient natural resources and capital. Also, even in the overpopulated nation, skilled and educated technicians and industry foremen were in short supply because young people went to college with subtle disdain for manual or technician's work, as they learned from a class-sensitive society. However, even from the ashes and stone age conditions created by the Korean War, the invaluable resource of people and brain power were there to face the challenges of social, political and economic revolution. Within the short period of time since liberation in 1945, the founding president Syngman Rhee started a courageous and visionary policy of land reform for farmers without land and the education of people by building public schools and colleges, and foremost inaugurating anti-communism, free democracy based on the market economy. The necessary stepping stones for the nation's industrialization was already set for Park to utilize.

Park made it a priority to attend a monthly export meeting and saw a drastic increase in export items and volume to his great relief. In the export trade, the first emphasis and priority went to the volume of trade, dollar amount of sale and not the profit, regardless of the manufacturing costs. The big objective was to establish themselves as an export country with the belief the profit would follow as the export continued. For companies which achieved the export goal for the month, for the quarter, for the mid-year and for the year, Park made sure to present the plaque of achievement with a token of celebration money, as in the army giving out medals to improve morale and as an example for others to follow. The effective technocrat mindset and the military competitiveness were everywhere in the government-guided economic development and industrialization to fulfill the age-old prayer to eliminate the dehumanizing and degrading poverty that might serve as a womb of communism.

Park's office in the presidential Blue House and the Economic Planning Board became the situation room for the war against poverty by making export the supreme marching order of the nation. The effort for exporting and manufacturing of products was not always stressful as people involved had occasions to celebrate reaching the goals or surpassing, with plenty of sake and karaoke songs deep into the night as soldiers after the long march sat around and sang popular songs together laughing and screaming with happy relief. "We can do" was their belief and starting with a meager $40 million export in 1961, the year of The 5.16 Revolution, to $100 million in 1964 and then $10 billion in 1977, then reaching the impossible, with exports of $538 Billion in 2014. Korea is now the 5th largest exporter in the world.

The sailing of the export business and economic development was not all with tailwinds. A strong headwind blew in 1973 when an unexpected catastrophe arose, the Yom Kippur War In the Middle East. The oil-producing Middle Eastern countries got together to unleash pressure on Western industrial powers supporting Israel with an oil embargo. The oil embargo happened at the worst time for South Korea, just starting the transformation of the economy to the heavy chemical industry requiring affordable energy and oil. The price of oil jumped overnight to drive out and kill the start-up industries in their cradles.

Nevertheless, the warriors for economic development in the government and private Industries did not sit idly by and lament the situation they did not cause to happen. Courageously, they got up to find a solution and sought to use the dilemma as a tonic shot to find more long-term energy solutions. They refused to take it as a poison to kill the patient, the Korean economy. The warriors had strong common sense to reason that cash-rich Middle Eastern countries with far more money than at any time in their history would want to use the money for improvement of the long-neglected social, economic and military infrastructures like housing, roads, bridges, airports, prisons, petrochemical plants, harbors, and military bases.

Koreans were right there standing on an acre of diamonds with overseas construction experience in Thailand and elsewhere and highly trained technical staff and especially those veterans retired from Vietnam ready for mobilization. Countries like Saudi Arabia, Libya, Iraq, and Iran liked Korean construction companies for their "Turnkey type construction" at a competitive cost and schedule to deliver the projects on time. Beside, Korea was the only country to commit a large group of disciplined workers in record time. Also, work done by Korean companies had the Korean government's guarantee and it was a no-brainer for Korean companies to get massive projects as one of the biggest export items. Construction contracts and labor supply business created not only a new export item of overseas construction but also generated extraordinary revenue and access to oil.

The new export of construction knowhow and the team became a savior for the nation to get out of the dilemma of oil shock and continue the planned reconstruction of the country. Eight billion dollars of revenue was earned from the overseas construction projects in 1978 alone. The widening and expansion of the "export first" policy of Park Chung-hee's government caused many obvious or subtle changes and transformations in people's lives and businesses. Traveling *botari* salesmen, bag people, slowly disappeared and major conglomerates started a new network- and client-based global marketing approach to sell more sophisticated and higher-profit export items, often with manufacturing facilities constructed in the host countries to help their own employment and economy.

Steel is an indispensable part of any manufacturing and industrialization. Korean economic leaders called steel "the rice of industrialization" as rice is the main and the most important food for a meal and survival in Korean society. Park and the economic planners all wanted a steel plant that could supply the steel needs for manufacturing and subsequent industrialization. However, the steel plant was hard to build as it was one of the most sophisticated and capital-intensive ventures and highly competitive globally. Many U.S. steel plants did not do well because of the international competition and cheap supplies from third world countries like China which, under modified communism with a capitalistic approach, had newer and more efficient plants to produce steel. In this background, Korea wished for its own steel plants. It was just a wish for a long time until Park had the visionary determination to build POSCO. He believed POSCO would put Korean industrialization on the firm and unbreakable foundation for the country to leave behind the unglamorous defeatism reminding one of the title "the ghetto,". Park's unflinching determination to provide the " rice " of the industrialization was firm and unshakable, but warning signals kept coming.

For instance, Korea's own economic planning board reported that estimated demand for steel might not justify its risk of investment to build a whole new steel plant. The steel demand within the nation would not be sufficient enough to support the scale of POSCO and the timetable of completion. Furthermore, the international authority on economic development policy and loan, IBRD (International Bank for Reconstruction and Development) recommended that the feasibility of a new steel plant was not there as the international surplus of steel existing from the old steel plants in the U.S. and countries in Europe and the emerging People's Republic of China would be sufficient unless a war broke out. IBRD also cited that similar steel plant projects started in other countries were unsuccessful because of sophistication of the plant and pollution control systems requiring major capital investment.

The project lost initial steam. A major departure from the initial plan followed to reduce the size and sophistication just to meet the reduced goal of replacing the import. Yet, the revolutionary mindset of the government planning experts came to rescue the original ambitious goal of building a ranking steel plant in Asia and the world with new project feasibility analysis and project justification. First, the feasibility analysis took the top-down approach rather than the bottom-up approach. In the bottom-up approach, potential demand for steel was determined by what was needed while the top-down approach was by what would be produced by the new steel plant. In other words, for the bottom-up approach, demands were given and the supply was the determinant while for the top-down, supply was given and demand was the determinant.

Simply put, in top-down, the idea was to produce X amount and to find ways to use that X amount profitably. Build the plant first, and worry about how the surplus product would induce new demands by new manufacturing or by export. This approach was very unorthodox but Park and his economic planners believed with conviction the common wisdom that " Where there is a will, there is a way." They also found similar logic in the Expressway that when constructed, traffic would follow. The increased traffic-carrying capacity increased travel desire and soon the increased traffic volume justified the original Expressway design and construction. Steel plant construction was no exception as long as the economy would expand as planned. Steel plant construction was a matter of collective determination and persistence to make the plan happen. The leader's determination and persistence helped to keep the original ambitious project intact for POSCO. Park urged his followers, "*an doe myun, doe ge ha ra.*" "If it doesn't work, make it work."

Rommel House on the dust-covered, wind-blown lot in Ulsan started to serve as headquarters for the first world-scale steel plant in Korea. The name of Rommel House was the logical choice of the diehard and determined warriors mobilized to the desert-like landscape, reminiscent of the desert fox, General Rommel of Nazi Germany, directing tank battles on the African desert front with heroic leadership and strategy. Their mission was not tank battles but had a similar intensity and concentration to build the first operational steel plant in Korea for manufacturing and export without depending on foreign imports. Again, Park's strong hands and clear direction as a technocrat were there to take a giant step for the nation's industrialization with a big chunk of the seed money and hope of all people attached. The hurriedly fabricated two-story building was what Rommel House looked like, but the house was buzzing with people with blueprints in hands and with unmistakable determination in their eyes. The house was lit brightly and people in grey uniforms and hard hats were in and out 24 hours a day at all times, rain or shine.

The workers had the almost impossible mission to design, construct and operate the steel plant POSCO with a big investment of the borrowed money. The success or failure of Rommel House would have a direct effect on the fate of the lofty goals of national industrialization. Rommel House sent groups of smart engineers to Japanese steel plants to learn and research the necessary knowhow of the construction in 1968. Japan's steel plants initially cooperated with Korean engineers on the field trip to make design drawings and the data available. Soon, Japanese companies worried about having potential competitors nearby and put up a high wall impossible to climb over for critical design data for the plant to build. Korean engineers returned without the blueprint of the plant to construct, but they were determined to develop Korea's own technological skill by doing more aggressive and comprehensive research. Korean engineers called on and contracted with steel plants in other countries, especially in the U.S. with many old steel plants, a remnant of their industrialization.

For this mission impossible, Park handpicked a military officer, Park Tae-jun, one of Park's students at the Korea Military Academy and known for his no-nonsense, results-oriented leadership. Under POSCO president Park Tae-jun's leadership and painstaking follow-ups, the collective effort had a break. After much trial and error effort, day and night, rain or shine, finally the plant was finished in 1973 without people knowing if it would live up to their expectations. All project-related people, top to bottom, gathered nervously to witness if their plant was a success to produce molten iron ore. Breathless moments passed and after a small initial trace of the liquefied iron, the brilliantly colored molten iron flowed. There was a moment of dead silence but soon, shouts of joy erupted like a chorus: "*Mansei, mansei*, long live the Republic of Korea!" Some people were weeping openly with a sigh of relief. The shouts of joy covered the entire steel plant and the waiting nation on a long trail of pain and poverty.

Korea successfully developed the world-scale steel plant by their own skill and technical ingenuity. From its humble beginnings at Rommel House, the shipbuilding industry and auto manufacturing started and now Korea is world #1 in shipbuilding in annual tonnage and # 5 in auto manufacturing, exporting Korean-made ships and automobiles to remote corners of the world. One of every other oceangoing ship was made in the small country of Korea wedged between China and Japan and a bulwark of free democracy and market economy.

Pony, the first Korean-made cars, were exported to Colombia, Venezuela and Ecuador in South America in 1976 and 40 years later people can see many Korean-made cars on the roads of the world cities. In fact, in Beijing, China, Hyundai limousines are conspicuous as people use them as yellow cabs. More milestones of industrialization were established for the once poor and abject nation. In 1980, Korea became the top household appliance-exporting country, in 1983 the first 64 KD semiconductor was invented, and in the same year the income per capita broke $10,000. In 1986 there was an economic surplus for the first time, and in 1988 the Olympics in Seoul with its grand finale impressed the world.

Korea has an outstanding cultural heritage and many scientific achievements. Nevertheless, long Confucian-influenced monarchs, brutal Japanese colonial rule and the devastating Korean War started by communists had left many negative collective traits of factionalism, character flaws, bribe-taking and corruption in government offices and people. Koreans gained notoriety as the best warriors for infighting among their own people and the worst in fighting outside invaders. The handling of the IMF(International Monetary Funding) crisis was exceptional with unity and persistence to overcome the national disgrace and to witness the improvement of people's collective morality by discarding the old negative traits from monarchs, colonialists and communists.

While pursuing Revolution and driving for industrialization and modernization, the country generated many firsts in the world. Shipbuilding #1, IT #1, Smartphone technology #1, semiconductor #1, LCD monitor #1, MP3 R&D #1, Inchon International Airport service and air freight #1. Besides, education and literacy is #1 and a surprising number of Korean immigrants and expatriates spread over the world is #1 too as a ratio of the population, numbering eight millions overseas. Also many industries in Korea have a commanding position in the world including: auto manufacturing, human robotics, high-speed rail, steel production and nuclear capability. Korea has twenty nuclear power plants and ability if required to make a nuclear bomb in six months.

In the middle of all economic and social progress in Korea in Park Chung-hee's tenure, one thing stands out, his character. Park was a technocrat with the mission to reconstruct the poorest country in the world. Park's character of honesty, patriotism, and a can-do spirit helped him to fulfill his mission in a most brilliant and charismatic way. Park had the most qualifications to usher the country into the world as a developed and aid-giving country. His humble birth, strong self-image nurtured by his mother's uncommon devotion, his military training from both militaristic Japan and the technocratic U.S., and his willingness to die for the country made him great. Without Park Chung Hee, Korea's industrialization was nothing but a dream, an illusion and an impossible dream. Park made the dream real.

WHAT STARTED WITH A SWORD

"Spit on my grave!"

Park Chung-he may be the greatest revolutionary in Korean history. He changed the backward and poor landscape of the nation and the people's mind-set and was on a fast-approaching course collision with destiny.

Hindsight gives perfect vision by eliminating the clouds of assumptions, expectations, and strong emotional attachment to the historical events happening. Park Chung-hee was not perfect nor was the Revolution. Many expectations and desires of people went astray and unfilled. Yet, historical landmarks in social, political and economic fields were made beyond anyone's doubt or suspicion during his leadership. Did real change come to Korea because Park Chung-hee spearheaded the revolution and led the export economy and industrialization in the face of accusation, opposition, and assassination attempts? He put his life and his family's future on the line when he pulled down the wing flaps of the malfunctioning plane, namely the Republic of Korea, for an emergency landing.

Furthermore, Park lost his wife at her prime of 49 years old by the bullet of a Korean communist living in Japan where freedom and openness were the norm. Park's commitment was to build a big ship, the Republic of Korea, in the deep waters and set a course of affluence and self-defense. In a dramatic way, Park succeeded and Koreans saw a glimpse of the peak that had been blocked by Korean's learned character defects: defeatism, factionalism, and self-deception. His belief in a "can-do spirit" and Koreans' survival capacity was remarkable when other rulers had failed to see them. Generations of self-doubt, *yup jun*, cheap Korean coins in contrast to strong Japanese "Yen" or the American "dollar" was gone, and in its place, people saw The Miracle on the Han River. Why? How? Has Park Chung-hee's unwavering and charismatic leadership and undaunting personal courage something to do with the success? Was Park a smart man with discipline too?

Park and the members of the Supreme Council for National Reconstruction bluntly stopped the zig-zag of the nation's course and planted not only tree seedlings to resurrect the green mountains but also implanted the can-do spirit throughout the mind of Koreans once colonized helplessly. The can-do spirit was inspired by Park's leadership and his example. Hindsight demonstrates that the spirit of "can-do" is not a mere product of his military training and his expert experience. It went deeper to the original source. The "can-do" spirit came directly to Park and then filtered to the nation's mind through Park's mother with unconditional love and supreme trust in her youngest son. Nature does not lie. Park's mother in the dilapidated farmhouse believed without a doubt that her son would do something meaningful and significant not only for him and his family but for the entire nation in shackles of colonialism in the near future. As the Korean adage goes, "When a bean is planted, a bean will come out."

"Small peppers are hotter." The age-old Korean saying could have been invented for Park Chung-hee. Not just hotter but the hottest pepper Koreans had ever tasted. Park was instrumental and pivotal in turning the wrong way of Korea to the revolutionary way for the elimination of chronic poverty and *Yupjun Eusik*, the self-defeatism. Park was smart and had the best qualifications to be the leader to change the country and create The Miracle on the Han River. From the ashes after the Korean War, the country became a developed country in the world and changed its position from aid-receiving country to aid-giving country because of Park's determination and visionary foresight. When the armistice of the Korean War was signed in 1953, the income per capita was a mere $67, the poorest country in the world and now the small country has become the 11th largest economy in the world with a GDP per capita of $34,386 in 2016.

Hindsight is a way to see a great man under full light without prejudice of the moment when the person lived. The real picture of the man will shine with more information on the person, the work, and special circumstances scrutinized more carefully after the person's passing. A gem or a pearl glitter more brilliantly when the mud and the dirt of conflicting interests and misconceptions are washed away by the cleansing water of time. The more time passes, the more objective and factual the character of the person becomes for all people, the old and new generation.

Since Park's assassination by his close friend and confidante the KCIA chief, Kim Jae-gue, in 1979, Park's personality, family, his career and mission as the industrialization president have been dissected, analyzed and evaluated by both his admirers and haters. Admirers consisted of the people who worked with him with direct and close contact everyday, and those who considered him as remote, forceful and a somewhat dictatorial political figure in the newspaper and mass media. Again, his haters included people in his proximity such as opposition political party leaders and people with close ties with communists or with a socialist bent. Those people were able to see Park's whole picture and his life, good or bad, true or not. But, one thing became clear. That was his influence and impact on people in the cities and rural areas as their lives became easier by finding jobs, gaining more income and having better places in which to live. Park made an indelible mark on people's lives in general.

People on the whole had the experience of living with less in despair because of poverty and lack of any major economic developments. They depended on foreign aid for survival. When the Third Republic under Park's leadership after the military revolution was established, people came to realize that the social order had returned, public work and business shops sprang up and genuine change of mood followed. Also, people noticed Park had a strong grip on the past and present of the nation bringing old unpunished political crimes and gangs to justice. Park's grip on the present was outstanding in clearing major stumbling blocks in the way of the economic development plan soon to be launched with all the money, people and force he could gather. The brown-colored mountains and hills with sparse trees and greenery drew attention from Park. All accepted that the use of the forest for firewood for cooking and heating was slowly but continuously destroying the once-beautiful mountains and streams. The look and destruction of mountains and forest were granted but not anymore.

The feeling of helpless abject poverty, a corrupt political system, and the scar of fratricidal Korean War were everywhere as a high-ranking U.S. official leaving Korea after the armistice lamented, " Don't expect a prosperous democratic country in Korea. It may take a hundred years. A rose won't bloom in the rotten waste." Where was the will for a national reconstruction to eliminate chronic poverty and to instill a can-do spirit which most citizens had given up on? The will came from the extraordinary life of devotion and persistence of Park. The will to turn the direction of the country from helplessness to hopefulness started to awaken as Park and the revolutionary government pushed the economic development plan with all their hearts. Soon, people realized how lucky the nation was to have such a courageous and determined political leader.

Park was persistent to complete what he started: the revolutionary goal of elimination of poverty; establishment of self-defense; and peaceful unification with economic power and not military force. Park realized with his keen sense of history and understanding of collective character flaws of Korean people that the Miracle of the Han River would not be easy. But, he would not allow the success of their bloodless revolution and the initial economic development based on surplus labor to go astray. He wanted to stay on course and to continue its successful direction of the country, live or die. Park understood that the bad colonial behaviors and the newly attained selfish habits from corrupt capitalism would not permit the normal healthy growth of free democracy and continued reconstruction of the country. As progeny saw, the combined forces of colonial misfits and murderous communists with false hope of utopia divided, lied, and devastated the hopeful bud of democracy and a political system of equality and wealth distribution. These misfits will never succeed to undermine the Miracle on the Han River because great patriots like Syngman Rhee and Park Chung-hee cared for the country of their birth.

Communist dictator Kim Il Sung of North Korea infiltrated many communist spies and the fifth column in South Korea and affected all branches of government especially judicial, legislative, and labor and education unions. Unusual disease requires unusual treatment to save the sick patient. Park detested the lies and propaganda of socialist-leaning groups among their midst with stealth assistance from the communists. These communist-inspired groups lived in a free democratic society but their true objective was to overturn the government with riots, agitation and division of people.

The so-called democratization movement with minor exceptions was anti-government and leaning to communism and they saw the defects of democracy so well and so magnified while they failed to see the wanton murders, imprisonment of people and enslaving of people as the worst combination of communism and Kim Il Sung's family succession of dictatorship. These imbalanced, ignorant groups saw the match fire well but chose to close their eyes to the volcano.

The North Korean regime, an evil combination of communism and family cult-like religion, has maintained indescribable crimes and inhumane dictatorship including: forced labor camps, restriction of people's movement, control of people's loyalty through the regimes' food rationing, requirement of a special pass to visit or move to the capital city, Pyongyang, punishment of three generations for one reactionary, mandatory self-critical meeting to control and enslave the general populace, a forced 90-degree body salute to over 34,000 of Kim Il Sung's and his son's statutes, state run of call girls to trap visitors from democratic South Korea, indoctrination of false ideology of "self-reliance" to keep 0.1 % of the ruling group in perpetual control and divine living, summary execution in the name of the people's court, and many more crimes and planned murders.

Park's leadership was strong and razor-focused on the Korean problems and he did not hesitate to initiate a revolution within a revolution to give the first-phase revolution a staying power to continue and fulfill the original goals. Park dissolved the assembly, the vinyl house of corruption and factional fighting and character assassination. Against the objection of the opposing party and the old revolutionary comrades, Park was forceful to push the *Yusin* constitution, the rejuvenation constitution, to fulfill the goal of the country's industrialization. *Yusin* was a revolution within a revolution to continue what he started. *Yusin* was a big departure from the 3rd Republic starting the 4th Republic to continue the economic development and the industrialization under perceived dangers in the nation. In the new constitution, dictatorial elements were included to enable Park to continue the industrialization and the national defense industry with the people's referendum. Park's painstaking analysis of the modernization in other countries, especially in Singapore, the Philippines and Japan, gave him some moral justification for the revolution within a revolution. Exception to ordinary democratic rule was essential to complete the historical work until a trustworthy political party would be ready.

Of course, shock was expressed by the opposing party and their followers. The theory-oriented political science professors in the ivory towers and people involved in the democratization movement were up in arms against the new constitution and the new republic. A few who participated in the 5.16 Revolution with Park expressed strong objection with genuine concern for the democratic principles to follow. The objectors were all products of the democratic education system started by the founding president Syngman Rhee. That proved the education was on the right track to produce good citizenry principled in democratic ideals. Yet, many of the objections were extreme. They did not present an alternative plan for the nation under grave danger but provided complaints with good excuses. Many activists were leaning to socialism or communism under the name of democratization and communist ties. " Spit on my grave" was Park's sense of sacrificial patriotism in the face of opposition.

Park was fearful to turn over the economic development plan and the security of the nation to politicians corrupt and ineffective for other than factionalization and lining their pockets with bribes and nepotism. Presidency for life was possible under the new constitution but not automatic and it required the referendum, the will of the people. Besides the need for continued effort for industrialization at any cost, other serious factors drew Park's attention for the new constitution. The problem was the continuous belligerence of North Korea to unify the Korean peninsula under their style of communism with constant threat of invasion. In fact, the North sent an armed special commando of thirty-one well-trained suicidal troops over the DMZ to assassinate Park in 1968 and the communist captured Pueblo, the U.S. navy vessel, making the political environment conducive to dictatorial power to withstand outside attacks and the growing threat within and without.

Park's focus was on the guarantee of successful industrialization and ascertainable nation's security. He also desired, in the long run, a peaceful unification based on an indisputable economic strength and monopoly of world influence. At the time Park paid special attention to development models that might give reference points and examples of success of industrialization and defense of their country. Three development models were available for Park's review and digestion, including the Meiji Restoration in Japan, Lee Kwan Yew of

Singapore, and Ferdinand Marcos of the Philippines. All three development models had relevance to Park's search for a Korean solution. The Meiji restoration was an inspiring example he had studied many times as a young student at the teachers' school and as a cadet at the military academies. The history of Japan's national modernization was fresh in his mind. Park realized the spirit of national unity and the aggressive as well as drastic policies in Japan helped to attain the successful revolution. Meiji went against the entrenched old power source like the samurai class and ruling overlords that wanted the old rule and system. He found many similarities in the Korean situation but many different conditions also existed.

For instance, the Meiji era enjoyed the well-established samurai class as a mindset for honesty, justice and mutual trust which could be used as galvanizing forces to restore and institute the Western advanced technology and political system. Park felt sorry Korea did not have the same favorable conditions. In reality, Korea had unfavorable liability as a nation, the opposite of the samurai spirit. Still deep in his mind, Korea needed the time and drastic measures if he wanted to complete the revolution and its manifested goals as its principal participant.

Lee Kuan Yew showed honesty and transparency of leadership to sustain the support of the majority of people in Singapore which did not have resources and raw materials but did live under Japanese occupation. In a small island overcrowded and racially complicated, communism was a major threat at first using the same technique of lies, threats, and propaganda. Lee thought communism was not the right political philosophy to build a new nation that would bring security, safety and happiness to everybody on an equal and equitable basis. Lee found the communist philosophy that the end justifies the means created riots, violent demonstrations and shortages when he tried to have a coalition government established. Lee first wanted to work with communists but soon he completely abandoned his strategy and drove out communists from the main political arena with the help of his party and followers. Use of lies, false propaganda, and inhumane brutality to control the masses did not agree with Lee. Besides, the fake communist prophet of no god with all power and control of human lives did not sit well with the educated and wise leadership of Singapore with Lee at the very center for not a couple of terms but thirty-one years in office to steer the small nation to the firm ground of prosperity.

Ferdinand Marcos of the Philippines was another breed of political leader with strong leadership, intelligence, and boldness to pursue what he believed to change the direction of his country for the better. As a lawyer and military commander, Marcos fought the Japanese Imperial Army along with the U.S. Army and as a forceful leader built more schools, industries and anti-communist measures to keep communists at bay. Marco's legacy was tarred by corruption and the siphoning out of large sums of government money to foreign accounts his family controlled. They lived the high life, a bad example to ordinary poor people. Imelda Marcos, his wife involved in politics as mayor of Manila, was notorious for her three-thousand pairs of shoes when big segments of the population were below the poverty level. Marcos was in power eighteen years by declaring martial law and change of the constitution to continue his policies and programs. Park thought the drastic measures like Marcos's martial law approach could be a choice if the precarious economic development and national security became questionable for the nation's survival.

Park wondered if democracy could be on hold in a limited way if the economy that provided the power to democracy was lacking and grossly deficient like in Korea. Park thought economic development had to be in shape first, especially for developing countries, before real democracy filtered to the people. Without the minimum economic support, Park thought democracy could become the sound of a gong as he remembered the wrinkled face of his mother with the empty rice sack. Park held his hands tightly, murmuring, "we have to eat first before enjoying the fruit of democracy." He thought the economic development and the industrialization had to continue even if he was accused of being a dictator delaying democracy in the country. "Let people spit on my grave," his tightly closed lips parted a little.

Hindsight is a luxury enabling posterity to integrate relevant information at the time of President Park Chung-hee's living. All new information is filtered by parties with different interests and people evaluating him, sometimes critical, and other times totally approving. Everyone on the earth has unique character strengths and weakness learned or in the birth gene, and idiosyncratic behaviors hard to justify. Park was very effective and trustworthy in his chosen career as a teacher, a soldier, a thinker, and a revolutionary and eventually as the ruler of the country for eighteen years.

Park's effectiveness as a leader and president is important on two fronts. One was physical improvement and the other was mindset. The physical improvement was he effectively liberated Korea from chronic and abject poverty for the first time in its 5,000 year history and the fact is self-evident and there is no need for elaboration. The other was improvement in Koreans' mindsets. Park effectively freed Koreans from again chronic *Yupjun Eusik*, a second-class and can-not-do mentality. This included the defeatism and self-belittling masochism learned from long years of Confucian-guided Korean monarchs and then embedded under the skin from Japanese colonial indoctrination. Even the change of mindset is self-evident when Korea's economic and scientific achievement are in review. Literally, people in the world cannot avoid their contact of either Korean-made things, K-pop, Korean drama videos or Korean immigrants and expatriates spread all over the world, eight million of them.

Effective and successful people in politics, business and military have a few common denominators that make them effective. Five simple denominators among many include COISA by their first letters:

C : Common Sense
O : On-the-job training
I : Intelligence
S : Self-image
A : Ability to finish what one starts

Common Sense

Park as a leader of his professional fields, especially as the president during the industrialization of the country, displayed uncommon common sense. Anecdotes showing his use of common sense are abundant. For example, to obtain a loan, seed money to start economic development, the poor country Korea did not have any money in the national coffer. After an initial unsuccessful attempt to get loans from countries like the U.S. and Japan, Park had the common sense to approach West Germany as a potential loaner. As age-old Korean common wisdom says, " The widow best understands the widower." Park hoped there was a chance in West Germany. To Park, Korea and West Germany had the same political condition with a country divided by ideology. They were both devastatingly war-torn countries with rubbles of stones to start, and both countries had educated people eager to work. With a series of friendly negotiations and guarantees on the loan payback, Park was successful in securing a small loan. The wages of exported nurses and minors to Germany was collateralized to make the loan possible. Park used the money for the start of light manufacturing and export principled industries, the first step of the long economic development plan and eventually industrialization of the country that ushered in the Miracle of Han River. Park's common sense in this case was simple and brilliant.

Another example of interesting personal common sense Park displayed as the president of a poor country was his family's dining table. For a poor country without enough food to go around and many people starving, Park showed exemplary common sense. Park's order for the dinner table was mixed rice was to be served, as white rice was in shortage and priced high for common people; no more than five side dishes; no food crumbs left in the dishes. The simple and honest example at the president's dinner table helped people share the food shortage until the planned economic development would resolve it. The common sense at the family dinner table at the presidential mansion was far-reaching. Maybe it was more than common sense. It was a character strength as an honest leader.

Another example of common sense was when the plot of the revolution was leaked to the Prime Minister Chang Myun, the highest office in the government, by the arrest of one of the key plotters two days before the D-Day of the revolution. It was a catastrophic leak that could have wiped out the revolutionary plan. When Kim Jong Pil, the Secretary General of the secret Military Revolutionary Committee, brought him the news and asked him what to do, after a moment of thought, Park's curt answer was "Push as planned." He added that God would wait for two days if their revolution was any good, and that the arrested plotter might withstand the interrogation for two days without further leak. Common sense to push his plan rather than a last-minute change of the plan saved the revolution.

On-the-job-training

Park had the most qualifications to be a leader living in his chosen fields as he had combined training in Japan's military ethos, and American effectiveness in technology. Because of his affiliation with military academies, he had the luxury of being trained on modern educational topics by top-notch instructors in a systemically organized way. Early training to be a teacher and working experience as a teacher in Korea colonized by Japan was important for Park's character-building and his association with smart Korean youngsters at the time. Besides, Park's eighteen years of comprehensive military service and training in the Republic of Korea army gave him a rare opportunity of holding various job assignments in intelligence, artillery, military supply command, chief of staff positions and commanding position of units including the army division. Park even had six months' training at the general staff college for artillery in the U.S.A.

Park also had actual battle experience during the brutal and nasty Korean War involving multiple nations on either side with responsibility to direct, train, and order troops to the life and death battle fronts. The experience in the bitter fratricidal war gave Park a razor-sharp focus on his mission, allegiance, and eventually the framework for the bloodless revolution to turn the tide of Korea's destiny from hunger and self-defeatism to prosperous free democracy. Park dreamed that South Korea would be ready to unite the country with economic power not with guns and tanks. As a technocrat, Park realized the importance of on-the-job training(OJT) more intensely and accurately than the most bureaucratic officeholders in the government agencies. During the industrialization phase of the economic development, Park went directly to a technical person on the job regardless of their rank to assess their project and to implement project elements for a successful conclusion. Park's approach sometimes created awkward moments for high bureaucrats with political skill but without necessary technical knowhow. These bureaucrats ended up losing sleep to study and learn things that were technical in nature to not look stupid with their high titles and education.

Also, Park initiated the opening of many technical high schools for youngsters who could not go to college because their family could not afford it financially. Good technicians were what the nation needed to show manufacturing capability to foreign investors and businesspeople setting up small shops in Korea to take advantage of excellent technicians and their low wages. Park's technocratic approach convinced many economic leaders around him that for the country's industrialization, technical skills in sequence had to be developed for high school graduates first. For instance, skills by hand first, and then skills by machine, skills by design, skills by system and finally skills by research were the logical order to follow. Making wigs for export by *Gongsuni*, young girls with minimum technical skill and schooling, next, electrical parts by *Gongdori*, young men with a high school certificate. Then, with confidence accumulated, making TV and household appliances by engineers, manufacturing cars by system specialists, and finally making smartphones by researchers followed in expedited speed. All went hand in hand. It was clearly inadvisable to skip steps and sequence for the overall scheme of national industrialization, the supreme objective of the nation within reach for the first time.

Park inspired technical high school students to compete at technicians' Olympics and get gold medals to induce foreign companies to come to Korea and open shops using Korean young boys to manufacture their company products to make money while creating jobs for Koreans. Park with understanding of OJT often invited scientists, engineers and PhDs from technologically advanced nations like the U.S.A., Britain, France and Japan, especially Koreans with higher education, to form the very foundation for industrialization. KIST (Korea Institute of Science and Technology) , KAIST, (Korea Advanced Institute of Science and Technology) were good examples of Park's qualification of OJT.

Intelligence

Intelligence is a mark of great and successful people but over the presence or lack of it the person has not much control. One has intelligence or does not. But how to use the given intelligence may depend on the real intelligence one may have. Many people do not have an adequate amount of intelligence to accomplish great things. Some people with intelligence do not know how to use it effectively but tend to squander or misuse it for wrong purposes, or for outright criminal things. Park was highly intelligent from his early childhood and held the class presidency every year in the elementary school under the Japanese education system. The class presidency was not by election but by appointment to the person who had the highest school grades. With intelligence and diligent work, Park made good transitions from elementary school to teachers' school and then Imperial Japan Military Academies with ease and promise.

Park's graduation records from military academies were excellent. He was the first of Japan Military Academy in Manchukuo and the second of the graduating class of Japan regular military academy in Tokyo, paving the way for potential leadership positions down the line. In very competitive military training, it would have been impossible to garner the honorable top positions as colonized subjects without a high degree of intelligence and a mental drive to support his work. The honors he earned helped him gain recognition and trust from contemporary Korean young students in the military institutions.

This recognition became a good personal resource for trust and collaboration on bigger matters affecting his life and death as seen in later years in the commutation of his death sentence from the military court and later in the forming of the military revolutionary committee. Park's remarkable possession and use of his intelligence to accomplish epochal economic development in South Korea were noted by the majority of Koreans, politicians and community leaders who cited him as a role model and mentor. Even outside of Korea, world-class political leaders lauded Park for his intelligence and courage in turning Korea's future direction. Deng Xiaoping of the People's Republic of China, who was instrumental in the adoption of capitalism for China's economic survival, had nothing but praise for Park as his role model. President Vladimir Putin of Russia openly admired Park for making the Miracle of the Han River possible. Putin gave a special order to his assistant to buy all the books on Park Chung-hee, showing his clear adoration and reverence. Some one hundred-sixty countries in Africa and elsewhere sent their community workers to learn the *Saemaul* movement in Korea for developing rural communities for better living and higher income, all because of Park Chung-hee's intelligence and ingenuity.

Success of the bloodless 5.16 military revolution was definitely another use of his intelligence in key decisions and detailed strategy of surprise and confusion. After consolidating revolutionary power with a new constitution, Park's intelligence was on full display in gathering all forces to embrace the greatest task of Korean history, the industrialization of the nation and the permanent elimination of poverty. Park's intelligence was so conspicuous in the reforestation of bare brown mountains that literally changed and restored the country with beautiful and majestic rivers and mountains. Economic winning-over of communist North Korea and the establishment of a national defense industry was another fine example of his intelligence to provide means for peaceful unification not by military force but by having military might as the deterrent. Park was born intelligent but he was more intelligent in using his intelligence as a patriot even though people complained that democracy was delayed.

Self-image

A man has an idea about himself. That idea of his ability and personality is a prime mover in his daily life. If all things are equal in a people's life, the person with a strong self-image always comes out as an achiever, winner, or leader. A strong and balanced mental picture often carries the day with faith in one's ability to face the reality and go forward to one's long-cherished goal. A strong self-image can make or break a man's life. Without a strong self-image, the man's long-range plans may easily stop mid-way towards the goal with plausible excuses that the weak self-image drums up. Park had a strong self-image nurtured by his devoted mother who paid more attention to her youngest son than she did to his other siblings.

Park's mother paid unusual attention to and love for the youngest son because she had the son at the very late age of 45 but also had guilty feelings for trying to abort him. The feeling of guilt completely reversed her attitude toward the son with devotion, trust and love that her son would grow up and accomplish something important and significant. Self-image can be equated with self-worth and Park had that feeling of self-worth that prevented him from being involved or mired in small petty things like taking bribes, nepotism, and mistreatment of his subordinates and poor people. Park's self-image and mental picture of self helped him in his pursuit of the bigger dream to eliminate degrading poverty in his loving country.

Ability to finish what one starts

Ability to finish what one starts is an important quality to achieve one's long-cherished goal. Likewise, one essential quality of a leader is his ability to finish what he starts. This simple truth is often overlooked to witness its catastrophic consequences. The importance of this staying power in business, academic research, military operations, and even athletic games needs no elaboration and emphasis. Until the final results of the plan, operation, and research come in, the initial individual efforts are in a state of flux with suspense and doubt about what will become of the original effort and participants of the goal. Without completing what he starts, his total effort at the start may become a waste, and worse, the reverse of the original plan may happen to harm those involved at the start and those who got on the bandwagon with hope and promises. Failure of completion of a worthwhile plan will hamper the next stage of actions and effort toward the completion of the overall goal. Park was endowed with the unquestionable ability to complete what he started. With sharp focus and uncanny ease, he was able to go from one step to another until finished with a tightly shut mouth and few words. Ability to complete what one starts is in large measure a learned habit.

Nothing is more true than that the habits form rapidly and effectively by intense training like a military academy learning environment and by experience in life-threatening brutal war with bayonet charges and the guttural sound of dying comrades. Like George Washington, the founding father and revolutionary of the American Independence War, Park had intense situations of life and death in war and the ideology of a divided country. The intense experience made Park a no-nonsense realist to complete his mission as George Washington endured seven long years to complete his mission which was improbable but inevitable with his revolutionary leadership. To complete his mission in the American Independence War, he stayed nonchalant until he saw the winning break by Providence or luck.

Park's training at the military academies within or out of Korea was not just weapons and battle strategy. It covered much broader subjects of learning that made him a well-rounded technocrat with a samurai spirit. Park was a good military commander and technocrat with comprehensive training and understanding of technology, numbers, and best of all, completion of given missions to lead the aimless Koreans from the desert of chronic poverty and defeatism.

With his character strength and love of the country, Park created the Miracle on the Han River and inspired a can-do spirit in Koreans. Look at the green mountains plush with fresh forests and beautiful streams as Park envisioned us to see.

Park Chung Hee accomplished what his loving mother expected, something important and significant. No one dares to spit on his grave as no one achieved what Park Chung-hee achieved visibly in peoples' pockets and invisibly in the mind of good Korean people with the mindset of "can-do".

NOTES

Preface

Page vii --- Hyundai Corp., a family-owned conglomerate, called a *Jaebol*, is a direct result of the successful industrialization of South Korea under Park Chung-hee. His goal was to liberate more than thirty million Koreans from abject poverty that had devastated people for time immemorial. Hyundai started as a small construction company to become a global company with the help of government policy and monetary support like Mitsubishi Corp. of Japan. See p. 45. For more details of any subject discussed here, refer to the INDEX.

Page viii --- Collective character flaw . Long colonial occupation and Confucian-guided monarchs of Korea caused a list of character defects for Koreans: bribery, dishonesty, defeatism, factionalism and *hantan juei*, a "one big deal" attitude.

Page x --- *Juche*, Self-reliance Symbolic national ruling principle concocted by the North Korean dictator Kim Il-sung to lure helpless populace to his dogma. Self-reliance has been an effective catchword to appeal to the people with painful experience of colonial subjugation. Kim used cunning propaganda to build his personal cult to perpetuate his dictatorship and family succession. Kim tried to undermine democratic South Korea by emotionally beseeching people in South Korea to go against any foreign presence, especially the U.S forces, an ally against possible communist attack.

Page xiii --- GDP (gross domestic product) of South Korea was $87 in 1961. South Korea was the second-poorest country in the world with less than the GDP of communist North Korea when Park and his revolutionary members launched the 5.16 Revolution. The country was in absolute poverty without natural resources and accrued capital for industrialization.

Chapter 1

Page 1 --- Kim Jae-gyu was Park Chung-hee's trusted friend and subordinate turned sole assassin who killed president Park in 1979. Kim was eight years Park's junior but they were from the same village and had a similar educational and military background. Park entrusted

Kim to the head of KCIA, the second-highest power position.

Page 1 --- Cha Ji-chul was a captain of the airborne paratroopers unit assigned with the mission to arrest the prime minister Chang Myun when the revolutionary troops occupied Seoul. Cha became a majority party assemblyman, then was appointed to be the head of the presidential guard unit after Yuk Young-soo, Park Chung-hee's wife, was assassinated by a Korean communist residing in Japan. Cha was assassinated along with Park Chung-hee by Kim Jae-gyu.

Page 2 ---1905-1910. Japan's early modernization enabled Japan to colonize the neighboring country, Korea, in a systematic and forcible way after winning two wars against Russia and China. Japan took away Korea's diplomatic right and military system first in 1905 and made all necessary social, economic and military preparation to annex Korea outright in 1910.

Page 3 --- Syngman Rhee was a Korean reformist at the end of the Joseon dynasty and a dedicated independence fighter for forty years in the U.S. Rhee tried to build bases and organizations in Hawaii and Washington, D.C. to support the Korean independence movement. As an educator and an ordained Christian minister, Rhee put emphasis on education to empower Koreans in America first. Rhee was elected to be the first president of the PKG, the Provisional Korean Government in Shanghai, China. After independence, Rhee was elected to become the founding president.

Page 4 --- The S. S. Gaelic. The first group of Koreans numbering 102 came to work at pineapple and sugar plantations in Hawaii in 1902 travelling by the steamship S.S. Gaelic to Honolulu. The small group became the nucleus of future immigration and the formation of the Korean community with schools and churches. Hawaii became the base for the Korean independence movement with Syngman Rhee at the center.

Page 11 --- Tinef. The famed physicist Einstein often sailed in Long Island Sound in a tiny boat named Tinef, "a piece of junk" in Yiddish, when he became a U.S. citizen. With his contribution to nuclear bomb construction, WWII ended in the U.S. and allies' victory, bringing about Korean independence.

Chapter 2

Page 14 --- Final testimony of Kim Jae-gyu at the military court hearing for the assassination of Park Chung-hee. Kim, in his testimony, asserted that his action was a revolution in itself to end Park Chung-hee's autocratic ruling of the country for worthy causes such as protection of democracy, prevention of casualties of demonstrators, and enhancement of Korea-U.S. relations.

Page 15 --- Meiji restoration was a epoch making event in Japan by modernizing the backward and weak country to defend itself against modern Western powers and to become a world power during the colonization era in the world. With the power from the Meiji restoration, Japan colonized Korea for thirty-six years. The economic development and industrialization in Korea started by the 5.16 military revolution used the Meiji restoration as a model for industrialization and modernization.

Page 15, 16 --- Kim Sin-jo. A survivor of the 31-man suicide commando sent by North Korea to assassinate president Park Chung-hee in 1968. All but two of the commandos were killed before their entrance to the Blue House, the presidential compound. North Korean dictator Kim Il-sung later made an excuse to downplay the attack by saying it was an attack without his knowledge.

Page 15 --- Export # 1. South Korea had been an import country for life necessities, appliances, tools, electronic and transportation vehicles, without a manufacturing industry. When the policy was announced, the obvious question was what to export from the second-poorest country in the world. With cheap labor, Park thought Korea could still export hand-mades, labor intensive items like wigs, dolls, and small souvenir items to start the export business.

Page 17 --- The 38th parallel is an infamous latitude line dividing North and South Korea causing human misery, family separation, and fratricidal war killing four million people on both sides. The demarcation line was established by agreement between the two WWII victors, the U.S.A. and the U.S.S.R., for their political and hegemonal interest.

Page 15, 68 --- Armistice of Korean War was signed in July 1953 just to stop the ferocious war of attrition without any guarantee of long term peace on the Korean peninsula and the Far East. The North Korean dictator unilaterally broke the agreement with an ensuing threat of attack on South Korea as Kim's economic plan did not work and his diplomatic standing in the world plummeted.

Page 21 --- 5.8 Plan was the original plan of the military by Park Chung-hee and the Military Revolutionary Committee in 1960 to remove president Syngman Rhee and the corrupt government. Student uprising on April 19, 1960, less than a month before the 5.8 plan, made the plan void.

Page 22 --- Yuk Young-soo was Park Chung-hee's wife, widely respected and admired for her grace and humility. During the belt-tightening economic hardship in Korea, she showed an example of diligence and modest living. She refused any personal bodyguards and freely went to many charity functions with encouraging words and actions.

Page 24 --- Gyeongbu Expressway project was the biggest construction project in 5,000 years of Korean history connecting two major cities, Seoul, the capital and Busan, the second-largest harbor city. The successful completion of the project at the least comparable cost and shortest time provided a catalyst for rapid economic development and industrialization as expressways in West Germany had done.

Chapter 3

Page 26 --- USAMGIK (United States Army Military Government In Korea) governed the south part of Korea as an interim government until the Republic of Korea was established on August 15, 1948 under the leadership of Syngman Rhee who was elected as the first president. USAMGIK provided security and order for the transition period which was violent, lawless and chaotic due to the direct confrontation of two diabolical political ideologies, democracy and communism. The interim care was ineffective due to the lack of local knowledge and native cooperation.

Page 29 --- "Little black boy" was the demeaning nickname of Park Chung-hee during his growing years at the elementary school. Park's humble physical endowment with short stature and dark skin made him popular with farmers and poor working-class people. Park's brightness and strong self-image helped him to stay in a leadership position from elementary school to the position of a president of a nation.

Page 29 --- The first son in Korean families used to have unequal treatment in the family circle as he was supposed to command a leadership position for family-related matters. The first son had more privilege than other siblings for material things and inheritance matters. But, he had more responsibility of family welfare and filial duty to take care of old parents, restricting his mobility and freedom of choosing a career.

Page 28, 29 --- In the primitive farming regions of Korea, pregnancy of a mother at the age of forty-five was rare and carried big responsibility for food and shelter of the newborn baby. The female life expectancy was less than thirty in 1917 when Park Chung-hee was born when his mother was forty-five.

Chapter 4

Page 37 --- Confucian influence in Korean monarchs during the five- hundred-year Joseon dynasty was crucial in shaping the country's social, economic and cultural conditions in passive and negative ways. Monarchs' dependence on Confucian ways made their ruling of the country easier and simpler but at cost of negative culture of military weakness and poverty-prone national policy of despising craftspeople, soldiers, and farmers.

Page 37 --- The rigid class division and autocratic governance of the Joseon dynasty created a big slave population in the country. Nearly half of the population were slaves depending on the masters for livelihood.

Page 39 --- Hermit Kingdom. Lack of military power for the nation's security and fear of foreign invasions made the Korean dynasty close their doors to the modernized western countries and made them lose valuable time for learning technology and systems for self-sufficiency and national independence.

Page 40 --- Chronic poverty. Predominant dependence on farming in an overcrowded and mountainous country drastically limited economic growth and well-being of its population. The rigid monarch's rule based on Confucian philosophy further restricted the development of other food sources or farming technology and exploration of other natural resources from the seas and underground mining. This created chronic poverty for people causing lack of food, shelter and proper clothing.

Chapter 5

Page 43 --- Samurais. Japan had Confucian influence and a rigid social class division before the Meiji restoration. Samurais were at the top of the classes and they filled the leadership positions in society, drawing a government stipend. Samurais provided leadership and a strict honor code as warriors and not as scholars, helping the social system to be based on honesty and honor.

Page 46 --- Mitsubishi Corporation was one of the first products of Japan's modernization during the Meiji restoration to encourage private entrepreneurship. The Corp. started with three small boats and a more effective business system than the bureaucrats to expand their business in the international market. Japanese government saw the increase of employment and commercial activities because of private sector business. The Japanese government had policies and assistance to help private sector business to compete in the international market.

Page 48 --- The Bismarck government of Germany was a role model for the Meiji restoration of Japan. Japan opened its doors to Bismarck government leaders and their industrial experts to visit Japan and mentor Japanese counterparts for rapid economic development and modernization. Through their help, Japan started manufacturing, textile, and spinning industries. The Japanese government sent their government officials and industry representatives to Germany to learn the modern government and industry system and Western culture to apply them to Japanese society.

Page 52 --- The PKG, Provisional Korean government, was a direct outgrowth of the 3.1 independence movement in Korea in 1919. The PKG was established in Shanghai, China to fight for independence without resources. The PKG had no military forces to battle Imperial Japan and to join allied forces for World War II victory.

Chapter 6

Page 55 --- 1848 Communist Manifesto, one of the most influential political manuscripts, was prepared by two German philosophers Karl Marx and Friedrich Engels. It presented an analytical approach to class struggle and the problem of capitalism. The Manifesto promoted many revolutions and class warfare in Europe and worldwide.

Page 62 --- 1945. World War II ended in the allied victory. Japan surrendered unconditionally and left their occupied countries, including the Korean peninsula. Quickly the USSR and the US moved in with the 38th parallel as a demarcation line. The line was agreed upon by the two world victors to form the cold war front.

Page 62 --- Hwang Tae-sung. The collision of ideologies between the two men Hwang Tae-sung and Park Chung-hee from the same farming village in south Gyeongsang province before the division of the country. Hwang was a diehard communist and a friend of Park Sang-hee, Park Chung-hee's older brother. Hwang, an independence fighter during the Japanese colonial period, turned communist and came down from North Korea to contact Park Chung-hee in vain. Hwang was executed as a communist spy.

Page 66 --- Propaganda. Communist North Korea always engaged in the constant communist propaganda against South Korea to divide South Korean democratic society with anti-government plots, riots and espionage. Through propaganda, communists infiltrated South Korean labor unions, teachers' unions and politicians to destabilize democratic South Korea.

Page 67 --- "The ends justify the means" was a communist catchphrase to influence young communist recruits in South Korea to undermine the government for communist takeover. The unjustifiable dogma appealed to new communists in the South to concoct many anti-government activities including terroristic threats and destruction of law and order.

Page 67 --- The paradise communists expounded upon for new "change facings" is a convenient communist theory of classless, stateless utopia. Kim Il-sung, the communist dictator, had no concrete example to show but innumerable statues and a starving population in the prison camps in North Korea.

Page 69 --- Jachihoe was what the first president Syngman Rhee started for elementary students to learn democracy and the election process in homeroom classes. Rhee emphasized the education of people to free them from illiteracy and empower people to build a new nation with liberty and justice for all.

Chapter 7

Page 76 --- Stone Age. The Korean War was a barbaric and fratricidal war involving some twenty countries with more bombs dropped than in World War II including four million casualties on both sides. Korea on both sides of the DMZ became a heap of stones akin to the real Stone Age.

Page 77 --- POW. Allied forces in South Korea had a major

camp of communist prisoners of war. Problems arose when anti-communist POWs refused repatriation and did not want to go back to the communist north. South Korean President Syngman Rhee had the courage to release 17,000 POWs against the wishes of the U.S. and allied forces in Korea.

Page 84 ---Thousand sheeps. George Washington alluded to a thousand sheeps in the heat of the ragtag revolutionary war against Great Britain. He stressed the importance of leaders in crucial military matters by saying that it is better to have a lion leader and a thousand sheep than a sheep leader and a thousand lions. In the leading of a country, the same logic applied. See p 205

Page 85 --- The first president Syngman Rhee had a second exile when his government was toppled by a student uprising in 1960. Rhee refused firing against demonstrating students and quickly resigned. Rhee took his second exile to Hawaii where he had started Korea's independence movement. He died there 5 years later at ninety without realizing his hope to return to his beloved country.

Chapter 8

Page 95 --- 3,600 was the troop strength of the revolutionary forces to quickly launch the bloodless revolution on May 16th in 1961. The troops were from the crack airborne unit, marines and artillery unit on the periphery of the army's main operational channel for secrecy and rapid mobilization.

Page 97 --- Military academies Park Chung-hee attended were all available in Korea at the time of the Japanese colonial period and after the independence. Park was only one among Korean military leaders who attended Manchukuo Imperial Military Academy, Tokyo Imperial Japan Military Academy and Korea Military Academy. Attendance at all three gave Park a definite advantage for his recognition among military members and his association among influential commanders for organized operations like the military revolutionary committee by connecting any faction by region, affiliation and graduate years.

Page 98 --- Second Republic after the first Republic founded by Syngman Rhee had the opportunity to establish law and order, economic development and punishment of the corrupt political leaders of the first republic. From the start of the second republic, extensive political divisions and power struggles made the government weak and inept, creating causes for military revolution.

Page 104 --- Bloodless revolution was the clear intent of the military revolutionary committee as emphasized in the troop addresses by Park Chung-hee for the start of the revolution. Bloodless revolution was the highest form of military uprising and the revolutionary committee under Park Chung-hee's leadership realized the goal successfully. The bloodless revolution further removed the chance of civil war and the long drawn-out military operation.

Page 108 --- Revolt against seniors. A group of Korean military academy officers 8th class with Kim Jong-pil as their leader was sensitive to the corruption of politicians creating nepotism and breakdown of law and order. The group was also mindful of the corruption within the military for illegal profiteering and election-rigging. The group revolted against seniors in the military hierarchy demanding resignation of commanding officers. The action indirectly helped to form the military revolutionary committee with the revolting group as the core.

Chapter 9

Page 114 --- General Chang Do-yong was the Army Chief of Staff at the time of the 5.16 military revolution. He had the full support of the ruling second republic's political leaders. Gen. Chung's real intention for the military revolution was not clear. Chung's ambivalence helped the revolution as he was used as a cover to keep the secret and confuse authority.

Page 134 --- Calendar change was one of the glaring revolutionary changes from the old status quo of chronic poverty and defeatism. Old calendar dated back to the opening of the ancient Korean Kingdom called "opening of the heaven". The old calendar was cumbersome as the dates were different from the calendar of modernized Western countries. The calendar change to the Gregorian calendar was a big step to open up international business.

Page 137 --- Normalization of relations with Japan was a tough threshold to end the awkward relationship between Korea and Japan from the colonial era. For mutual benefit, both countries required normal relations for peace in the region and in the Far East and to form a regional alliance against new marauding communism. The U.S. as a superpower of democratic countries advocated and support the normalization.

Chapter 10

Page 140 --- Coal bricks with 19 holes were the traditional symbol of the Korean lifestyle. Korean families depended on firewood gathered from mountains for cooking and heating. As the population grew, collecting dried leaves of trees and cutting trees went deeper to mountains and became time-consuming and inefficient. Unrestricted tree cutting denuded the once beautiful mountain range and caused mudslides and forest fires. Park stopped tree-cutting altogether as part of the revolutionary policy and made people use coal bricks brought from coal mines with the government's support for transportation. The use of anthracite coal with plenty of deposits in the country became mandatory to preserve the nature and mountains.

Page 140 --- Firewood. As the South Korean economy grew with exponential growth of the GDP (Gross Domestic Product), the use of firewood gathered from the hills and mountains was completely replaced with alternative energy sources for cooking and heating. The replacement of firewood required remodeling of kitchens, bathrooms, sewer and water services. The new energy sources were coal, electricity, natural gas, oil and nuclear power bought with the additional income from industrialization. Replacement of firewood fundamentally changed the landscape of South Korea with lush green forests and peoples' modern lifestyle.

Page 142 --- Micro-farming was a typical farming practice for the majority of farmers with small tracts of land to support the family. The founding president Syngman Rhee was pivotal to enable micro-farmers to own their land through Land Reform improving their status from surf or contract farmers to independent farmers. Micro-farmers started to diversify into other crops, vegetable greenhouses and raising of domestic animals for additional income and commercialization.

Page 146--- Borigogae. The infamous words of fear of starvation disappeared from South Korea because of their miraculous economic development and industrialization. The words of Borigogae means a hill of barley to go over until the harvest of rice a few months later in Korea. The spanning of a few months' gap of grain shortage was treacherous and difficult causing malnutrition and starvation.

Chapter 11

Page 155 --- 5 year economic development plan, first started in 1962, was an ambitious blueprint for the economic development and industrialization of South Korea. Park Chung-hee as a well qualified technocrat was most influential in pursuing the plan with the U.S.-educated experts of economy for prompt plan adjustment and follow-through in logical and effective plan execution. The economic planning and its execution under the iron hand of Park Chung-hee's leadership made brilliant progress in a comprehensive, cooperative and continual way, creating the Miracle on the Han River.

Page 158 ---Export meeting. Park Chung-hee and his government had "export #1" as the prime marching order for the country. The president and responsible economic experts held frequent and continuing export meetings to encourage export business and to solve potential problems of money, labor and government regulations. Enormous effort was exerted to graduate from the unglamorous title of the second poorest country in the world. With an analytical plan, military discipline and undaunting courage, Park and his government ushered in an aid-giving power position to Korea as the world's 11th biggest economy.

Page 159 --- Cash-rich Middle-Eastern countries became a blessing in disguise for South Korea in 1974 during the oil crisis caused by the war in the Middle East. South Korea was undergoing national industrialization with prohibitive oil price increases. Park and his economic advisors, along with construction company executives, used the occasion to launch lucrative overseas construction businesses utilizing educated Korean workers and soldiers returning from their assignment in South Vietnam.

Chapter 12

Page 165 --- The Miracle on the Han River was a rare achievement by the nation without many natural resources or investment capital in an overcrowded, poor South Korea. Park Chung-hee was the unchallenged leader with a clear sense of direction and an uncommon combination of courage, discipline and technocratic skills responsible for the creation of the miracle. Park almost single-handedly was able to mobilize the entire nation without economic strength to fulfill his and the nation's dream to conquer absolute poverty and to create the Miracle on the Han River.

Page 169 --- No enrichment. Park Chung-hee's sudden death by two bullets from the pistol of his trusting subordinate, Kim Jae-gyu, the head of the KCIA, proved one thing beyond anyone's doubt, that Park was an honest leader without personal enrichment. Park had no Swiss bank account, no trust fund for his children, no hidden assets for anyone in his family. Park had no time to prepare for his death and no camouflage was possible. Park Chung-hee was the most honest president and he was focused on the nation's industrialization.

Page 178 --- Communism was a gray color of Park Chung-hee and many compatriots during the chaotic and violent period shortly after the independence in 1945 because of confrontation of two diabolical political ideologies in South Korea. Park's fuzzy red color of political belief proved to be the color of the most genuine democracy. Park won the war against communists economically by creating a strong economy forty (40) times stronger than communist North Korea and by laying concrete footing for peaceful unification.

Page 180 --- Park Chung-hee was the most effective ruler in five thousand years by liberating people from absolute poverty. Park represented a conglomeration of essential character traits and education to serve as a unique industrialization president when the nation needed it most. Park could assemble his strength as an educator, a soldier, a thinker, a philosopher and a revolutionary to mobilize the entire nation with an unflinching vision of Koreans' "can-do" and brilliance. Because of Park Chung-hee, South Korea became an independent and aid-giving country.

AUTHOR BIOGRAPHY

Young Lee was born in Korea. He spent his boyhood in Seoul, during the fratricidal Korean War. He attended the engineering college of Seoul National University (SNU). He served in the Korean army as a Lieutenant and worked as a Civil Engineer for Hyundai Corp. during the belt-tightening era in Korea. In 1967 at age 26, he came to New Jersey as an engineering trainee, attending New Jersey Institute of Technology (NJIT), achieving both a Masters and Doctor of Engineering Science degrees with a dissertation on applying systems technique to transportation engineering.

He later served as an adjunct professor at NJIT. Specializing in transportation infrastructure design and construction management, Young gained much experience at various consulting engineering firms, ultimately founding his own engineering company. As CEO, he spent the remainder of his professional career there until his retirement. He remains an active professional engineer and professional land surveyor, licensed in various states.

An avid student of meditation, but also physically active, Young enjoys kayaking, golfing, snorkeling, and swimming, all of which he has pursued during his travels to many states and countries. Proud father of two daughters and grandfather of three, he is a naturalized U.S. Citizen, residing in New Jersey and Florida with Kim, his soul mate, and wife of 50 years.

LEE YOUNG

BIBLIOGRAPHY

4.19 Revolution, Wikipedia, the free encyclopedia

Armstrong, Charles, "The North Korean Revolution, 1945-1950," Cornell University Press ITHACA and London, 2003.

Barkan, Elliott Robert, "Making it in America: A Sourcebook on Eminent Ethnic Americans," E.R. Barkan, editor, ABC-CUO, Inc. California, 2001.

Boyd, Arthur L., "Operation Broken Reed: Truman's Secret North Korean Spy Mission," Philadelphia, Da Capo Press, 2007.

B.B. Bonnie, editor, "Korea Under the American Military Government 1945-1948," Praeger Publishers, Westport CT, 2002.

Bozo, Adrian (2007). The making of modern Korea. Taylor & Francis.

Breen, Michael, "Syngman Rhee: President Who Could Have Done More," Korea Times, 2011-11-02.

Cha, Marn J., "Koreans in Central California (1903-1957): A Study of Settlement and Transnational Politics," University Press of America, Maryland, USA, 2010.

Choi, Sook Nyul, "Year of Impossible Goodbyes," Houghton Mifflin Co. New York 1991.

Chung, Henry, "The Case of Korea: The Case of Korea: A Collective of Evidence on the Japanese Domination of Korea, and on the Development of the Korean Independence Movement," Fleming Revell Co, New York, 1921.

Clark, Eugene Franklin, "The Secrets of INOTON," G.P. Putnams Sons, NY 2002. Colonialism - Wikipedia, the free encyclopedia https://en.wikipedia.org/wiki/Colonialism Communism - Simple English Wikipedia, the free encyclopedia https://simple.wikipedia.org/wiki/Communism

92nd Congress, 2nd session, committee print, "Communist Treatment of Prisoners of War," A Historic Survey, Committee on the Judiciary, United States Senate, Washington, 1972.

Coover, Robert, "The Public Burning," Grove Press, New York 1977.

Coppa, Frank J., ed. (2006). "Rhee, Syngman". Encyclopedia of modern dictators: from Napoleon to the present. Peter Lang. ISBN 978-0-8204-5010-0.

Cummings, Bruce (2010). "38 degrees of separation: a forgotten occupation". The Korean War: a History. Modern Library. ISBN 978-0-8129-7896-4.

Dallek, Robert, "The Lost Peace: Leadership in the Time of Horror and Hope 1945-1953," New York, New York, Harper Collins, 2010

Demick, Barbara, "Nothing to Envy: Ordinary Lives in North Korea," Random House Digital, Inc New York 2009.

Dillard, James E. "Biographies: Syngman Rhee". Korean War 60th Anniversary: History. US Department of Defense.

Dong, Stella, "Shanghai: Rise and Fall of a Decadent City," William Morrow, New York, 2000.

The Economic Planning Board, Economic policy of the development era: 20 years of the Economic Planning Board, 1982.

The Economic Weekly, A Journal of Current Economic and Political Affairs, June 20, 1953, "Syngman Rhee's Threat to Peace" Editorials. Economy of South Korea - Wikipedia, the free encyclopedia
https://en.wikipedia.org/wiki/Economy_of_South_Korea

Edward Mason, The Economic and Social Modernization of the Republic of Korea, Havard University Asia Center, 1980. Empire of Japan - Wikipedia, the free encyclopedia
https://en.wikipedia.org/wiki/Empire_of_Japan

Farivar Cyrus (2011), "The Internet of Elsewhere: The Emergent Effects of a Wired World", Rutgers University Press. Ferdinand Marcos - Wikipedia, the free encyclopedia
https://en.wikipedia.org/wiki/Ferdinand_Marcos

Fuqua Jr., Jacques L, "Korean Unification Inevitable Challenge," Potomac Books, Washington D.C., 2011.

Gaddis, John Lewis, "Cold War: A New History," Penguin Books, New York, 2007.

Ha, Jin, "War Trash," Random House Digital, Inc., Dec 18, 2007, P102, <huge number of nonrepatriates>

Haig, Alexander M, Gilbert Bill, "Ship of Miracle," Triumph

Books, Chicago 2000.

Halberstam, David, "The Coldest Winter American and the Korean War," Hyperion, NY 2007.

Han, T.I., "Lonesome Hero Memoir of a Korean POW," Authorhouse, Indiana, USA, 2011.

Harrison, Selig S., "Korean Endgame A Strategy for Reunification and U.S. Disengagement," A Century Foundation Book, Princeton University Press, USA 2002.

Hong, Sung-You, Korea Economy and the US Economic Assistance, Parkyoungsa, 1962.

Hong, Won Pyo, "The Comparative Study on the Political Thought of Rhee Syngman and Sukarno: Focusing on Arendtian Theory of Founding," Hankuk University of Foreign Studies, Seoul, Korea 2010

Hurh, Won Moo, "I Will Shoot Them From My Loving Heart." McFarland & Co., North Carolina, 2012.

Hyun, Peter, "Man Sei!: The Making of a Korean American," University of Hawaii Press, 1986.

Ienaga, Saburo, "The Pacific War 1931-1945," Iwanami Shoten, Tokyo, 1968.

Jager, Sheila Miyoshi, "Brothers at War: the Unending Conflict in Korea," W.W. Norton & Co. New York, London 2013.

Jessup, John E. (1998). "Rhee, Syngman". An encyclopedic dictionary of conflict and conflict resolution, 1945-1996. Greenwood Publishing Group. Joseon - Wikipedia, the free encyclopedia https://en.wikipedia.org/wiki/Joseon

Kang, Hildi, "Under the Black Umbrella: Voices from Colonial Korea, 1910-1945," Cornell University Press, Ithaca & London, 2001.

Kim, Byung-Koo, "Nuclear Silk Road," 2011.

Kim, Byung-kook and Ezra F. Vogel, ed. (2011). The Park Chung Hee Era: The Transformation of South Korea. Harvard University Press. ISBN 978-0674058200.

Kim, Elaine H; Choi, Chungmoo, editors, "Dangerous Women: Gender & Korean Nationalism," Routledge, New York, 1998.

Kim, Esther Ahn, "If I Perish," Moody Press, Chicago, 1977.

Kim, Grace Ji-Sun, "The Grace of Sophia: A Korean North American Women's Christology," Wipf & Stock Publishers, Eugene, OR, 2002.

Kim, Hakjoon, Syngman Rhee, Asianow, November 30, 2000.

Kim, Henry Cu, "The Writings of Henry Cu Kim," Edited and translated by Dae-Sook Suh, University of Hawaii Press, Honolulu, 1987.

Kim, Hyung-A (2003). Korea's Development Under Park Chung Hee (annotated ed.). Routledge.ISBN 978-0415323291

Kim, Joong-Seop, "The Korean Paekjong Under Japanese Rule: The Quest for Equality and Human Rights, New York, Routledge, Curson, September 1, 2003.

Kim, Joung Won, Divided Korea; The Politics of Development, 1945-1972, East Asian Research Center, Harvard University press, 1976.

Kim, Young Suh, "Wisdom of Korea," College Park, MD, Korea Times, "LA Riots," May 1992

Kramer, Gene obituary, March 11, 2011, Washington CAP

Lee, Erica; Yung, Judy, "Angel Island: Immigrant Gateway to America," Oxford University Press, 2010.

Lee, Kempeth B., "Korea and East Asia, The Story of a Phoenix," Praeger Publishers, Conn. USA, 1997. Lee Kuan Yew - Wikipedia, the free encyclopedia
https://en.wikipedia.org/wiki/Lee_Kuan_Yew

Lee, Soo-Jung, "Making and Unmaking the Korean National Division: Separated Families in the Cold War and Post-Cold War Eras" dissertation, University of Illinois, Urbana-Champagne, 2006.

Lee, Young, "Kayak to Serenity" PublishAmerica, Baltimore, 2012, ISBN 9781629078649

Lee, Young, "New Dawn" America Star Books,Baltimore, 2014, ISBN 9781611027693

Lien, Pei-te; Conway, Margaret, "The Politics of Asians: Diversity of Community," Routledge, New York, 2004.

Lynn, Hung Gu, "Bipolar Orders: The Two Koreas Since 1989," Fernwood Publishing Canada, 2007.

. Manela, Erez, "The Wilsonian Moment: Self-Determination and the International Origins of Anti-Colonial Nationalism," Oxford University Press, June 20, 2007 <Preview of 20 pp available>
Marguerite Powers, Charlotte (2010). "The Changing Role of Chaebol: Multi-Conglomerates in South Korea's National Economy" (PDF). Georgetown University. Retrieved 31 May 2016

Mason, Edward, The Economic and Social Modernization in the Republic of Korea, Cambridge, Harvard University Press, 1980.

May 16 coup, Wikipedia, the free encyclopedia, https://en.m.wikipedia.org/wiki/May_16_coup

McKenzie, Fred Arthur, "Korea's Fight for Freedom," New York, Fleming H. Revell Company, 1920.

McMahon, Robert, "The Cold War: a Very Short Introduction," Oxford Press, Oxford, 2003. Meiji Restoration - Wikipedia, the free encyclopedia https://en.wikipedia.org/wiki/Meiji_Restoration

Merrill, John, Korea: The Peninsular Origins of the War (University of Delaware Press, 1989).

Millett, Allan R. "War Behind the Wire: Koje-do Prison Camp," MHQ Magazine. Published online, January 20, 2009 Miracle on the Han River - Wikipedia, the free encyclopedia https://en.wikipedia.org/wiki/Miracle_on_the_Han_River

Monarchy - Wikipedia, the free encyclopedia https://en.wikipedia.org/wiki/Monarchy

"The National Committee for Investigation of the Truth about the Jeju April 3 Incident". 2008. Retrieved 2008-12-15.

Gen Paik, Sun Yup, "From Pusan to Panmunjon," Brassey's, Dulles Virginia, 1999.

Oh, Won Chul, The Korea Story: President Park Jung-hee's Leadership and the Korean Industrial Revolution, Wisdomtree, 2009.

Park, Chung Hee, The Country, The Revolution and I, Hollym Corporation Publishers, Seoul, Korea, 1970.

Park, Chung Hee, Our Nation's Path: Ideology of Social Reconstruction, Hollym Corporation Publishers, 1970.

Park, Chung Hee, To Build a Nation, Acropolis Books, Washington, D.C., 1971.

Park Chung-hee, Wikipedia, the free encyclopedia, https://en.wikipedia.org/wiki/Park_Chung-hee

Park, Chung-Shin, "The Protestant Church As a Political Training Ground in Modern Korea," International Journal of Korean History (Vol. 11, Dec. 2007).

Park, Ji Eun, "In Search for Democracy: The Korean Provisional Government," a thesis submitted for B.A. Wesleyan University, Middleton, Connecticut, 2009.

POW, THE FIGHT CONTINUES AFTER THE BATTLE: The Report of Defense's Advisory Committee on Prisoners of War, August 1955. Burgess, Carter L.

Pratt, Keith, "Everlasting Flower: A History of Korea," Reaktion

Books Ltd, London 2006.

"Syngman Rhee". South Korean President. Find a Grave. Feb 20, 2004. Retrieved Aug 19, 2011.

Rhee, Syngman (2001), The Spirit of Independence: A Primer for Korean Modernization and Reform (translated with an introduction by Han-Kyo Kim), Honolulu, Hawaii: University of Hawaii Press, ISBN 978-0-8248-2349-8

Rose, Lisle A., "The Cold War Comes to Main Street," University Press of Kansas, Lawrence, Kansas, 1999. Saemaul Undong - Wikipedia, the free encyclopedia
https://en.wikipedia.org/wiki/Saemaul_Undong

Seo, Jung-Seok, "President Syng-Man Rhee and the Confucian Culture," Seoul , Sung-Kyun-Kwan University.

Shin, Jong Dae, Christian F. Ostermann, and James F. Person (2013), North Korean Perspectives on the Overthrow of Syngman Rhee, Washington, D.C.: North Korea International Documentation Project

Svada, Andrea Matles; Shaw, William, "South Korea," Diane Publishing, Federal Research Division Library of Congress, Washington D.C., 1997.

Tirman, John (2011). The Deaths of Others: The Fate of Civilians in America's Wars. Oxford University Press. pp. 93–95. ISBN 978-0-19-538121-4.

Tudor, Daniel, "Korea: The Impossible Country," Turtle Publishing, VT, USA, 2012.

Watkins, Yoko Kawashima, "So Far From the Bamboo Grove," William Morrow & Co, New York 1986.

Winters, Jeffrey A., "Oligarchy," Cambridge University Press, New York, 2011.

Woolley, John and Peters, Gerhard, "The American Presidency Project at UC Santa Barbara," California USA, 1999.

Yoo, Young-Bok, "Tears of Blood, A Korean POW's Fight for Freedom and Justice," translated by Paul T. Kim, createspace, USA, 2012.

You, Jong-Sung, "Embedded Autonomy or Crony Capitalism ?, Explaining Corruption in South Korea . . .," Harvard University, paper prepared for the annual meeting of American Political Science Association, September 2005.

Yu, Beongcheon, "Two Pioneers, Han Yong-un & Yi Kwang-su,

of Modern Korean Literature," Wayne State University Press, Michigan, 1992.

Zaide, Gregorio, Ph.D., "WORLD HISTORY IN ASIAN SETTING," REX Printing Company, Quezon City, Phillipines, 2000.

Video Links:YouTube
About Park Chung Hee – talks by Armstrong, Sorensen, Vogel
Economic Globalization: Documentary on the History of Economic Globalization
Korea, China & Japan The History that Unlocks the Future
Korean History Time Map
The Milacle of the Han River – Park Chung Hee
One Man's Vision: How Park Chung Hee Changed South Korea
An Overview of Korea
The Park Chung Hee Era: The Transformation of South Korea
Park Chung-hee Audiopedia
Park Chung Hee Legacy
Reassessing the Park Chung Hee Era, 1961-1979
Secrets Behind Korea's Economic Success
Singapore's Founding Father
Smart City: Seoul, Korea
South Korea Documentary HD ENG
Speech of President Marcos during the termination of Martial La, January 17, 1981
The Ties That Bind Japan & Korea

LEE YOUNG

INDEX

59990802R00139

Made in the USA
Middletown, DE
27 December 2017